HAPGOOD

by the same author

ROSENCRANTZ AND GUILDENSTERN ARE DEAD
ENTER A FREE MAN
JUMPERS
NIGHT AND DAY
THE REAL THING
TRAVESTIES
DALLIANCE and UNDISCOVERED COUNTRY
(a version of Arthur Schnitzler's *Das weite Land*)
THE REAL INSPECTOR HOUND and other entertainments
(After Magritte; Dirty Linen; New-Found-Land;
Dirty Linen (concluded); Dogg's Hamlet, Cahoot's Macbeth)
ROUGH CROSSING and ON THE RAZZLE
ARCADIA

Screenplays
ROSENCRANTZ AND GUILDENSTERN ARE DEAD: THE FILM
THE TELEVISION PLAYS 1965–1984
(A Separate Peace; Teeth; Another Moon Called Earth;
Neutral Ground; Professional Foul; Squaring the Circle)

Radio Plays
THE PLAYS FOR RADIO 1964–1991
(The Dissolution of Dominic Boot; 'M' is for Moon Among Other
Things; If You're Glad I'll Be Frank; Albert's Bridge;
Where Are They Now?; Artist Descending a Staircase;
The Dog It Was That Died; In the Native State)

Fiction
LORD MALQUIST AND MR MOON

HAPGOOD
TOM STOPPARD

ff

faber and faber
LONDON · BOSTON

First published in 1988
by Faber and Faber Limited
3 Queen Square London WC1N 3AU
Reprinted with corrections 1994

Typeset by Parker Typesetting Service, Leicester
Printed in England by Clays Ltd, St Ives plc
All rights reserved

A CIP record for this book is available from
the British Library

ISBN 0-571-19857-0

2 4 6 8 10 9 7 5 3 1

For Oliver with love and thanks

We choose to examine a phenomenon which is impossible, *absolutely* impossible, to explain in any classical way, and which has in it the heart of quantum mechanics. In reality it contains the *only* mystery . . . Any other situation in quantum mechanics, it turns out, can always be explained by saying, 'You remember the case of the experiment with the two holes? It's the same thing.'

Richard P. Feynman
'Lectures on Physics'/'The Character of Physical Law'

CHARACTERS

HAPGOOD	aged thirty-eight
BLAIR	probably twenty years older, but in good shape
KERNER	forty-ish
RIDLEY	mid-thirties
WATES	either side of forty-five
MAGGS	twenties
MERRYWEATHER	twenty-two
JOE	eleven
RUSSIAN	any age, thirty to fifty

ACT ONE

Scene 1   The Pool, Wednesday morning
Scene 2   The Zoo, Wednesday noon
Scene 3   The Rugby Pitch, Wednesday afternoon
Scene 4   The Office, Thursday morning
Scene 5   The Shooting Range, Thursday afternoon

ACT TWO

Scene 1   The Office, Thursday evening
Scene 2   The Studio, Friday morning
Scene 3   The Zoo, Friday noon
Scene 4   The Office, Friday afternoon
Scene 5   The Hotel, Friday evening
Scene 6   The Pool, Friday night
Scene 7   The Rugby Pitch, Saturday afternoon

Hapgood was presented by Michael Codron at the Aldwych Theatre, London, on 8 March 1988. The cast was as follows:

HAPGOOD	Felicity Kendal
BLAIR	Nigel Hawthorne
KERNER	Roger Rees
RIDLEY	Iain Glen
WATES	Al Matthews
MERRYWEATHER	Adam Norton
MAGGS	Roger Gartland
JOE	Christopher Price *or* Andrew Read
RUSSIAN	Patrick Gordon

Directed by Peter Wood
Designed by Carl Toms
Lighting by David Hersey

ACT ONE

SCENE I

We are looking at part of the men's changing room of an old-fashioned municipal swimming-baths. It is ten o'clock in the morning. The cubicles are numbered, and they have doors which conceal occupancy although they don't meet the ground. There is a wash-basin or two, a place to shave facing front. Four of the cubicles have to 'work'.
There are four ways of coming and going: 'Lobby', 'Pool', 'Showers', and, for the sake of argument, 'Upstage'.
The lobby doors have MEN *in reverse on the glass. Signs saying* POOLS, SHOWERS, GENTS *and* EXIT *may be used.*
One of the showers is evidently in use – we can hear it. When we encounter this scene, WATES *is shaving. He is a black man, an American, who is normally impressively tailored and suave but at present is dressed in cast-offs and looks as if he spent last night on a park bench. His tackle is basic – shaving brush, shaving stick, old-fashioned safety razor.*
Before anything else happens we have a short radio play. What we can hear is two people (a man and a woman, HAPGOOD) *talking to each other on shortwave radio. The voices have a slight distort.*

RADIO: OK, we have a blue Peugeot . . . stopping.
     Single male.
     It's not Georgi.
     Anybody know him? No briefcase, repeat negative on
     briefcase.
     Are you getting this, Mother? – we have the Peugeot but it's
     not Georgi.
     He's crossing the road. Fancy tracksuit, running shoes. No
     sign of the follower. Are you getting this? – target is
     approaching, negative on Georgi, negative on briefcase,
     negative on follower, give me a colour.
HAPGOOD: (*On* RADIO) Green. You should be seeing Kerner.
RADIO: Negative. They changed the plot. Confirm Green.
HAPGOOD: (*On* RADIO) Green. Tell me when Kerner shows.
WATES: (*Live*) If he shows.

I

HAPGOOD: (*On* RADIO) Tell me when Kerner shows, he'll be walking.

WATES: (*Live, no emotion*) Kerner is thirty thousand feet up on Aeroflot, I feel sick.

RADIO: Who *is* that?

HAPGOOD: (*On* RADIO) Wates – just shave.

WATES: (*Live*) Yes, Ma'am.

RADIO: Target inside. Negative on Kerner. Target in lobby. Ridley has seen him. Still negative on Kerner. Do I hear yellow? Mother, give me a colour, we're still – OK, we have a walker.

OK, we have Kerner . . . three hundred yards . . . affirmative on briefcase.

Target's got his key.

HAPGOOD: (*On* RADIO) Say when.

RADIO: Four – three – two –

(*The lobby door opens.*)

You're looking at him.

(*A* MAN *enters from the lobby. He wears a colourful tracksuit and running shoes. He carries a towel rolled up into a sausage, we assume the swimming trunks and cap are inside. He carries a key on a loop of string which might make it convenient to wear as a pendant. He is otherwise empty-handed. We call this man* RUSSIAN ONE, *because he is Russian and because there are going to be two of them.*

RUSSIAN ONE *enters Cubicle One.* [*This numbering has nothing to do with the actual numbers on the cubicles, it is only for our convenience.*] RUSSIAN ONE *enters his cubicle and closes the door behind him.*

RIDLEY *enters from the lobby. He is carrying a briefcase* [*but the briefcase may be inside a sports holdall.*] RIDLEY *now goes on a perambulation. The essence of the situation is that* RIDLEY *moves around and through, in view and out of view, demonstrating that the place as a whole is variously circumnavigable in a way which will later recall, if not replicate, the problem of the bridges of Konigsberg* [*and which will give* RUSSIAN ONE *time to undress*]. *Back to the plot.* RUSSIAN ONE, *dressed to swim, leaves his cubicle, locks it, swings his towel up and over the lintel and*

*leaves it hanging there, and goes off to the pool. When he has
gone* RIDLEY *posts his briefcase under the door of Cubicle One,
and pulls the towel off the door.* [*As a matter of interest, the*
RIDLEY *who posts the briefcase is not the same* RIDLEY *who
entered with it.*] RIDLEY *enters Cubicle Two and closes the door
behind him. The towel appears, flung over the lintel, hanging
down.* WATES *continues to shave. The shower continues to run.*
KERNER *enters from the lobby. He carries a briefcase. He has a
towel and a key. He looks around and posts his briefcase under
the door with the towel showing* [*Cubicle Two*]. KERNER *pulls
the towel off the door and tosses it over the door into the cubicle.*
KERNER *enters another cubicle* [*Cubicle Three*] *and closes the
door behind him. A moment later his towel appears over the lintel.*
RIDLEY *leaves Cubicle Two, bringing* KERNER's *briefcase with
him, and also the towel. He chucks the towel over the door of
Cubicle One. With the briefcase he disappears in the direction of
the showers. The shower cubicle may be in full view, in which
case we see* RIDLEY *delivering his briefcase to the occupant.*
RUSSIAN ONE *leaves the pool, wet of course, and re-enters his
cubicle.*

RIDLEY *comes back into view, from the showers, without the
briefcase. He goes to the pool.*

RUSSIAN TWO *enters from the lobby. He is the twin of* RUSSIAN
ONE, *and dressed like* RUSSIAN ONE. *He carries a similar
rolled-up towel. However, he also carries a briefcase. He glances
round briefly, and notes the towel on Kerner's door* [*Cubicle
Three*]. *He posts his briefcase under Kerner's door. He enters a
cubicle, Cubicle Four.*

MERRYWEATHER, *a boyish twenty-two-year-old in sports jacket
and flannels, enters from the lobby. His manner is not as well
calculated as* RIDLEY's *had been. He is at first relieved and then
immediately disconcerted by the absence of Russians.*

RUSSIAN ONE *now dressed, leaves his cubicle, carrying his
rolled-up towel but leaving the briefcase* [*which Ridley posted*]
behind. RUSSIAN ONE *leaves to the lobby.*

MERRYWEATHER, *whose idea of making himself inconspicuous
has been, perhaps, to examine himself in* WATES's *mirror,
follows* RUSSIAN ONE *out to the lobby.*

3

KERNER, *dressed, leaves Cubicle Three, with the briefcase which had been posted there, and leaves to the lobby.*
RUSSIAN TWO *reappears, from Cubicle Four, and enters Cubicle One to collect the briefcase which had been posted there by Ridley. As he leaves the cubicle,* RIDLEY *re-enters from the pool.*
RUSSIAN TWO *leaves to the lobby.* RIDLEY *follows him out.*
WATES *has finished shaving. He is packing up his shaving tackle. The shower stops running. There is a pause, and then the occupant of the shower,* HAPGOOD, *approaches, somewhat encumbered by a briefcase [Kerner's original] a leather rectangular clutch handbag with a shoulder strap, and an umbrella which she is at the moment taking down and shaking out. From her appearance, the umbrella has been an entire success. She comes down into the light and leans the umbrella carefully against the cubicles, and stands pensively for a moment. She is apparently too preoccupied to acknowledge* WATES, *who is himself preoccupied with something which makes him shake with silent laughter. He is putting a heavy steel wrist-watch on his right wrist.* [NOTE: *All the foregoing action may be done to music and lightly choreographed.*])

WATES: Young guy in a sports coat, college haircut, nasty wart on the back of his right hand, no, left, it was in the mirror.

HAPGOOD: Merryweather.

WATES: Merryweather, right. Followed the man in, followed the wrong man out, meanwhile Merryweather's man turns around and leaves with the goods. Sort of dummy.

HAPGOOD: Yes, he is rather.

(*The lobby doors open.* RIDLEY *enters in a somewhat excited, even delighted, state.*)

RIDLEY: (*Greeting her*) Mother.

HAPGOOD: This is Ridley.

RIDLEY: You didn't tell me it was twins.

HAPGOOD: This is Wates.

(HAPGOOD *puts the briefcase on the ground, then lays it flat. She undoes the catches and raises the lid. During this* WATES *and* RIDLEY *shake hands.*)

WATES: Ben Wates.

RIDLEY: (*Friendly*) Ridley.

(HAPGOOD *has stood up, taking from the case a flat white*

4

*cardboard box, a few inches square, the sort of thing that might
contain a computer disc, which is what in fact it does contain.
However, she is not the slightest interested in the box. She stands
staring down at the open briefcase.)*

HAPGOOD: (*Bad news*) Wates.

(*Now* WATES *looks at her and at the briefcase.*)

WATES: Oh, Lord.

HAPGOOD: Where's yours, Ridley?

RIDLEY: In the Peugeot.

(MERRYWEATHER *returns, looking sheepish.* HAPGOOD *tosses
the disc-box back into the briefcase.*)

MERRYWEATHER: Sorry, Mother – I –

HAPGOOD: Where did he go, Merryweather?

MERRYWEATHER: Actually, I lost him – a taxi came round the
corner –

HAPGOOD: He's in the taxi?

(MERRYWEATHER *nods.*)

RIDLEY: (*To* HAPGOOD) Chamberlain's cab, I love it. Listen, how
the hell –

HAPGOOD: (*Politely*) Be quiet, Ridley.

(*She is opening her handbag and taking out a small radio
transmitter/receiver.
These gadgets are going to get quite a lot of use and evidently the
state of the art has arrived at a radio which is no larger and
somewhat slimmer than twenty cigarettes. The radio speaks
quietly.*)

(*To* MERRYWEATHER) Have a look round the pool.

MERRYWEATHER: Right. What for exactly?

HAPGOOD: Anything there is, I'll want to see it. (*To* RADIO)
Cotton.

RADIO: Mother.

(WATES *and* MERRYWEATHER *dovetail with* HAPGOOD *and
her radio.*)

WATES: (*Shaking hands*) Ben Wates.

MERRYWEATHER: How do you do, sir? Merryweather.

(MERRYWEATHER *goes out to the pool.* RIDLEY *is probably
contemplating the briefcase.
*WATES *moves quietly up towards the cubicles and calmly*

investigates them, one after another without fuss. During this:)

HAPGOOD: (*To* RADIO) Where is he?

RADIO: In the Peugeot.

HAPGOOD: (*Patiently*) Thank you, Cotton, and where is the Peugeot?

RADIO: Camden High Street.

HAPGOOD: Pick him up and I want everything, I want him in a plastic bag.

RADIO: Yes, ma'am.

HAPGOOD: Contents of briefcase. I'm here to be told.

RADIO: You know it's twins?

HAPGOOD: Yes, I know it's twins.

> (*To* RIDLEY) You take Kerner – go through him, do it properly.
>
> (*To* RADIO) Chamberlain.

RIDLEY: Kerner's clean.

RADIO: P.O.B.

HAPGOOD: (*To* RADIO) I know.

RIDLEY: I did the switch.

HAPGOOD: (*To* RIDLEY, *more sharply*) Move.

> (RIDLEY *exits to the lobby.*)
>
> (*To* RADIO) Where are you?

RADIO: Chalk Farm, turning west on Adelaide.

HAPGOOD: Bring him in.

RADIO: Say again?

HAPGOOD: Just do it.

RADIO: Okay, guv.

HAPGOOD: Taxi needs back-up.

RADIO: (*New voice*) Roger.

HAPGOOD: I'm here to be told.

> (*She turns the gadget off, hesitates, and turns it on again.*)
> (*To* RADIO) Paul . . .
> (*Her tone for Paul is different – she is not giving orders. No answer.*)
> Paul . . .
> (*Still no answer. She turns the radio off.*
> WATES *is coming back to her.*)

What are you thinking?

6

WATES: I guess we took our eye off the ball.

(HAPGOOD *closes the briefcase.*)

HAPGOOD: What happened to the bleep?

WATES: (*Shrugs*) It's dead.

HAPGOOD: I'll need when.

WATES: You'll get it. Why did he take the film?

HAPGOOD: Who?

WATES: Yeah, that's the other thing.

(HAPGOOD *goes to collect her umbrella.*)

HAPGOOD: (*To* RADIO) I'm leaving.

RADIO: Car out front.

HAPGOOD: (*To* RADIO) Thank you.

(*She puts the radio back into her bag.*)

Wates . . .

WATES: Yes, ma'am.

HAPGOOD: Thank you for your co-operation.

WATES: You bet.

(*He holds the briefcase out for her and she takes it.*)

HAPGOOD: Well, we'll talk. You're invited.

WATES: Appreciate it.

(HAPGOOD *starts off to the lobby door.* MERRYWEATHER *comes back in from the pool.*)

MERRYWEATHER: Nothing, Mother – the whole place is clean.

HAPGOOD: (*Continuing out*) Drain the pool.

(*The doors swing shut behind her.*)

MERRYWEATHER: (*Thoughtfully, not entirely happy*) Drain the pool.

(*He goes back to the pool.* WATES *is alone. He is evidently a man with a burden. He is getting ready to leave, perhaps he has a coat to put on. From the pocket he takes a similar radio and walks towards the doors, raising the radio to his mouth; at which point everything changes for him. He stops to listen, his head turned back towards the upstage, by which time, gracefully and without making a big thing of it, he has tossed his radio from right hand to left, and produced from somewhere about his person a short-barrelled revolver. He stands listening, holding the gun down by his side. He has to be patient but after a while a figure comes out of the dark upstage between the cubicles. This turns out to be a*

7

*man wearing a hat and a good tweed overcoat, his hands in the
pockets, a slightly surprising colourful silk scarf tucked inside the
coat. He walks down in his own time, a careful stroll.* WATES
does not move until the downstage light falls across BLAIR's *face.*
BLAIR *comes to a halt.* WATES *puts his gun away, gets the radio
back into his right hand and resumes.*)

WATES: (*To* RADIO) Wates – I need the sweeps. (*He nods at*
BLAIR) Paul.

BLAIR: (*Greets him back*) Ben.

RADIO: Sweeps coming up.

WATES: (*To* RADIO) Thank you.

(*He puts the radio in his pocket and, in leaving, speaks to* BLAIR
without reproof, just information.)
She blew it.
(*He goes out through the lobby doors.* BLAIR *takes a radio from
his pocket. The scene begins to change.*)

BLAIR: (*To* RADIO) Ridley.

RIDLEY: (*On* RADIO) Ridley.

BLAIR: (*To* RADIO) I want Kerner in Regent's Park, twelve
o'clock sharp.
(*He puts the radio away and looks at his wrist-watch. The next
time he moves, it is twelve o'clock and he is at the Zoo.*)

SCENE 2

KERNER *has been brought by* RIDLEY *to the Zoo.* BLAIR, *having
checked the time on his watch, nods at* RIDLEY *to dismiss him.*
RIDLEY *moves out.*
Perhaps we are looking at BLAIR *and* KERNER *through the bars of a
cage. There could be a bench, there could be paper cups of coffee . . .
The bars make hard-edged shadows. We need one particular and
distinct demarcation of light and shadow on the floor, perhaps thrown
by the edge of a wall.*
KERNER *speaks with a Russian accent, which is not too heavy; in
fact, attractive.*

BLAIR: You're blown, Joseph.

8

KERNER: I love it. You blew it and I'm blown: well, I'll be
blowed. Nobody teaches that, you know. They teach you so
you can almost read *David Copperfield* and then you find out
David talks like a language student, he must have been put
in as a sleeper.

BLAIR: Well . . . you're blowed, Joseph. Your career is over.

KERNER: Except as a scientist, you mean.

BLAIR: Yes, that's what I mean.

KERNER: My career as your man at the Pool.

BLAIR: Or theirs. Just an observation. The meet at the pool came
unstuck this morning. We have to consider you blown as our
joe. The Russians must consider you blown as their sleeper.
Either way your career is over. *Which* way, is perhaps an
academic question.

KERNER: And yet, here you are.

BLAIR: One likes to know what's what.

KERNER: Oh, you think there's a what's-what? Your joe. Their
sleeper. Paul, what's-what is for zoologists: 'Oh yes –
definitely a giraffe.' But a double agent is not what's-what
like a giraffe, a double agent is more like a trick of the light.

BLAIR: Joseph –

KERNER: Look. (*He points.*) Look at the edge of the shadow. It is
straight like the edge of the wall that makes it. This means
light is particles: little bullets. Bullets go straight. They
cannot bend round the wall and hit you. If light was *waves* it
would bend round the wall a little, like water bends round a
stone in the river.

BLAIR: (*Irritated*) Yes. Absolutely.

KERNER: So that's what. When you shine light through a gap in
the wall, it's particles. Unfortunately, when you shine the
light through *two* little gaps, side by side, you don't get
particle pattern like for bullets, you get wave pattern like for
water. The two beams of light mix together and –

BLAIR: Joseph. I want to know if you're ours or theirs, that's all.

KERNER: I'm telling you but you're not listening. Now we come
to the exciting part. We will watch the bullets to see how
they make waves. This is not difficult, the apparatus is
simple. So we look carefully and we see the bullets, one at a

9

time. Some go through one gap and some go through the other gap. No problem. Now we come to my favourite bit. The wave pattern has disappeared. It has become particle pattern again.

BLAIR: (*Obliging*) All right – why?

KERNER: Because we looked. Every time we don't look, we get wave pattern. Every time we look to see how we get wave pattern we get particle pattern. The act of observing determines what's what.

BLAIR: How?

KERNER: Nobody knows. Somehow light is continuous and also discontinuous. The experimenter makes the choice. You get what you interrogate for. And you want to know if I'm a wave or a particle. Every month at the pool, I and my friend Georgi exchange material. When the experiment is over, you have a result. I am your joe. But they also have a result: because you have put in my briefcase enough information to keep me credible as a Russian sleeper activated by my KGB control; which is what Georgi thinks he is. So naturally he gives me enough information to keep me credible as a British joe. Frankly, I can't remember which side I'm supposed to be working for, and it is not in fact necessary for me to know. (*Pause.*)

BLAIR: It wasn't Georgi today.

KERNER: No?

BLAIR: No, it was different today.

KERNER: Today you decided to look. Why was that?

BLAIR: Some of your research has turned up in Moscow. Real secrets, not briefcase stuff.

KERNER: Tsk, tsk, tsk.

BLAIR: That's what the Americans said, roughly.

KERNER: The one shaving.

BLAIR: Mm. Ben Wates, CIA. You'd appreciate him, he makes waves with a Smith and Wesson.

KERNER: I'm sorry, Paul.

BLAIR: (*Shrugs*) Cousin-trouble is nothing new. This thing with you is trouble, though. Oh yes. If the Evil Empire has a tap into *you*, that's quite another ballroom as Wates put it –

KERNER: Ballgame. I think.

BLAIR: I assure you it wasn't. Ballpark. Anyway, Wates flies in and says, 'I have come from Washington to help you. How about Kerner for a start? Do we know anything about Joseph Kerner?' Well, we do as a matter of fact. He's Russian from Kaliningrad. The Russians put him in as a sleeper years ago but we turned him round and now he's really working for us, they only *think* he's working for them.

KERNER: What did he say?

BLAIR: He said: you guys.

KERNER: Poor Paul. What happened at the Pool?

BLAIR: Wates wanted us to abort the meet and put you through the mangle. But Mrs Hapgood insisted you were straight. And she wanted to keep the channel open. She made Wates an offer. She duplicated the contents of your briefcase. So now we had everything twice, in two briefcases. Ridley showed up before you at the Pool –

KERNER: What is a mangle?

BLAIR: I'm trying to tell you what happened at the Pool.

KERNER: You already did. Your Mr Ridley delivered to my Russian control and I delivered where Ridley put his towel. Quite nice. If I'm putting something extra in my briefcase, you get it all back.

BLAIR: That sort of thing.

KERNER: And was there something extra in my briefcase?

BLAIR: No. There was something missing. The computer disc was there but the films were gone.

KERNER: A puzzle.

BLAIR: Now we come to the exciting part. Wates had booby-trapped your briefcase. He sprayed the inside with an aerosol can, like radioactive deodorant – did you ever hear of such a thing?

KERNER: An isotope solution. If I open the briefcase I give a Geiger reading.

BLAIR: Yes, Wates shakes your hand and he has a counter which goes on the wrist and looks like a Rolex. We're working with people who tried to kill Castro with an exploding cigar. It's a joke shop.

KERNER: So, did I give a Geiger reading?

BLAIR: No.

KERNER: (*Pleased*) Oh, good.

BLAIR: We also had a bleep in your briefcase.

KERNER: A bleep?

BLAIR: A radio transmitter.

KERNER: Oh – a *bug*.

> (BLAIR *gives him a look.*)

> Sorry. A bleep in my briefcase. Go on.

BLAIR: Wates tracked the signal all the way to the meet. There the signal died. And the transmitter went missing from the briefcase, which nobody opened. The job was done by Mr Nobody.

KERNER: Well I'm blown. Blow me for a monkey's uncle. Can I say that?

BLAIR: I would avoid it. Any thoughts, Joseph?

KERNER: Mr Nobody put something extra in my briefcase. Then he found out my delivery was going to be intercepted. So he had to take it out again.

BLAIR: But why remove our rolls of film? He'd only have to take out what he put in, and we'd be none the wiser.

KERNER: Obviously because he put *in* a roll of film and they all look the same; he had to take them all.

BLAIR: (*Pause*) Obviously. By the way do you know anything about twins?

KERNER: Twins?

BLAIR: That was the other thing. It wasn't Georgi today, it was twins.

> (KERNER *laughs.*)

> Yes, that's my favourite bit too. Give it some thought. Will you?

KERNER: Oh, yes. But excuse me, now it is time for the feeding of the seals.

> (KERNER *strolls away, jerking his head at the unseen* RIDLEY *to follow him.* RIDLEY *re-enters and follows* KERNER *out at a comfortable distance.*
> BLAIR *stands looking out front. The next time he moves he is on the touch-line of a rugger pitch.*)

BLAIR *is standing in an open exterior against a grey sky on a cold October afternoon. He is watching thirty eleven-year-old boys playing rugby. This, alas, is not as rich in sound effects as one might think: There is the referee's whistle, there are occasional piping exhortations to 'Heel', 'Drive', 'Shove', and so on, and the occasional sound of the ball being kicked, but much of all this is happening at a distance, and so the general effect is sporadic anyway. Nevertheless it would be nice to work out where* BLAIR *is before the next thing happens – which is that* HAPGOOD *comes hurtling crabwise and in full cry along the touch-line. She is shod and dressed for the conditions and is carrying a boy's two-piece tracksuit, the top half of which is perhaps tied round her neck. Her momentum takes her a good way along the front of the stage, passing in front of* BLAIR.

HAPGOOD: Come on, big shove now, St Christopher's! Heel! –
      break! . . . well tackled, darling! – I mean, Hapgood – oh,
      sugar . . .
      (*The match recedes but she always gives it as much attention as
      she can spare or as she is allowed.*)
      Look at their little knees. Don't you love little boys?
BLAIR: It's never been encouraged in the Service. Which one is
      he?
HAPGOOD: The handsome one.
BLAIR: Oh, yes.
HAPGOOD: Don't wave.
BLAIR: I wasn't going to.
HAPGOOD: I used to wave. He told everyone he was adopted. You
      are nice wearing the scarf, you don't have to.
BLAIR: I like the scarf. I wanted to see you –
HAPGOOD: – wanted to see *you* –
BLAIR: – before you see Wates. Washington wants –
HAPGOOD: Kick! – kick for touch! – oh, sugar! –
      Tackle! – tackle low . . .
      (*Referee's whistle. Bad news for* HAPGOOD.)
      Oh . . . Bad luck, St Christopher's! Little darlings, they look
      so cold. Sixteen love.

BLAIR: Nil. Washington wants us to take Kerner off everything.

HAPGOOD: What have the Americans got against Kerner?

BLAIR: Well, this is just an educated guess but I suppose if they're going to spend a hundred million dollars over here on Kerner's SDI research they'd rather he didn't continue swapping briefcases with the high dive champion of the Russian Embassy.

HAPGOOD: Paul, Kerner is my star.

BLAIR: Means nothing.

HAPGOOD: Do you want me to tell you or not? I had six months' work in Kerner's delivery, long-term reflectors on countdown.

BLAIR: Do talk English.

HAPGOOD: Disinformation that had to be launched, I couldn't *afford* to abort the meet just because Washington got into a flap about Kerner.

BLAIR: You can't blame Washington. Kerner's pure gold, the man with the anti-particle trap, and if he's leaking his own stuff to Moscow we're making it awfully easy for him.

HAPGOOD: Kerner's all right – I run him and he's just doing what I tell him.

BLAIR: Wates made the same point. Don't take it personally.

HAPGOOD: Why would I? It isn't personal.

(*The referee's whistle – the conversion of the try.*)

Eighteen. Come on, St Christopher's! Lets get one back! This is personal. Everything else is technical. You're personal sometimes; but not this minute which is all right, so what can I tell you? – it isn't Kerner.

BLAIR: So what happened at the pool? It's a technical question, it almost looks as if you could solve it with pencil and paper: cubicles A, B, C, D, briefcases P, Q, R, find X when the angles are Kerner and the Russian twins, which is a question in itself – are these the famous KGB twins? Now that's what I call a double agent. Who's in charge and is he sane?

HAPGOOD: I hate it, Paul.

BLAIR: Yes, why aren't we pleased?

HAPGOOD: It reeks. The KGB twins are like an old joke that

keeps coming back, we've been hearing it for years and I never believed it. And suddenly here they are, identical and large as life. I hate it. (*Pause.*) But it's about the twins. The answer. I nearly got it, then I lost it.

BLAIR: Do you want to keep them for a while?

HAPGOOD: No – chuck 'em out. They're stooges, Paul. The meet this morning went exactly as the Russians planned it, including the arrests. The twins were expendable, they were meant to be seen, they were a success – 'Now he's here, now he's there, oh my God, there's two of them!' Wates nearly cut himself shaving he was so fascinated. He's doing a diagram, on pink paper, showing who was where when, all the coming and going.

BLAIR: He showed me. Guess who was holding the briefcase when the transmitter went off the air.

HAPGOOD: Who was?

BLAIR: You were.

(*Referee's whistle – a try is scored.*)

Our side isn't doing too well. Well, if it's you I don't care which side traps its particles. Anti-particles. Do you know what they are? They were never mentioned by Democritus who was the pro-particle chap when I was at school.

HAPGOOD: When a particle meets an anti-particle they annihilate each other, they turn into energy – bang, you understand. You can produce anti-particles in a collider and bottle them in a magnetic field but then you're stuck – the bottle is as big as a barn, and when you open the door you've got a billionth of a second so you have to be quick. If you could slow them down enough to get hold of you'd be in business, and Kerner thinks he can. Do you want me to tell you how?

BLAIR: You know, I don't really . . .

HAPGOOD: (*Shouts*) Break! Blind!

BLAIR: . . . I gave a chap a job with us once because he said he'd read physics and I thought he meant the book by Aristotle.

HAPGOOD: Was that last try converted?

BLAIR: No.

HAPGOOD: You weren't looking.

BLAIR: They re-started with a drop-kick.

HAPGOOD: Joe's worried about something too, we've both got the same look.

BLAIR: I've lost him again – you can't tell one from the other when they're all in the same get-up.

HAPGOOD: Once when he was really little, he got unhappy about something, he was crying, he couldn't tell me what it was, he didn't *know* what it was, and he said, 'The thing is, Mummy, I've been unhappy for *years*.' He was only as big as a gumboot.
(*Pause. She freezes, thinking.*)
Oh . . . ssh – sugar! – Paul, you just said it.

BLAIR: What did I?

HAPGOOD: You can't tell one from the other when they're all in the same get-up. That was what it was. Listen. Ridley's by the pool, Ridley's Russian is getting dressed. Merryweather's Russian arrives. Merryweather follows his Russian in and he follows the other Russian out, and why not? – they're identical and he only saw them one at a time, it could happen to anybody, especially to Merryweather, he probably still doesn't know there were two of them. Now Ridley comes from the pool and the same thing happens to him. He followed one Russian in and he follows the other one out, and why not? – they're identical and he only saw them one at a time. Then he comes back inside and he says, 'You didn't tell me it was twins.'
(*Referee's whistle, a longer one indicating the end of the game.*)
It's true. I didn't.
(*Distantly the two rugby teams call for three cheers for each other, first for St Christopher's, secondly for St Codron's.*)

BLAIR: So how did he know?

HAPGOOD: He was expecting twins. I think it's Ridley, Paul. I've left my own back door open.
(*Clapping*) Well played, St Christopher's . . . bad luck –

BLAIR: Oh, f-f-fiddle!
(JOE *enters.*)

HAPGOOD: Hello, darling.

JOE: Hello, Mum.
(*He is very muddy and glad to see her. His boots are a size too large.*)

HAPGOOD: Bad luck – well played anyway. Put this on.

JOE: Thanks.

(*He takes the tracksuit and puts it on.* HAPGOOD *helps him a little.*)

BLAIR: Hello, Joe. I'm afraid they were rather good, weren't they?

JOE: Yess'a.

BLAIR: How are you otherwise?

JOE: All rights'a, thank-yous'a. We always get beaten. I wish you wouldn't watch, Mum.

HAPGOOD: Well, I like watching, I don't mind if you get beaten.

JOE: But nobody watches except you.

HAPGOOD: There's lots of people watching – look over there.

JOE: That's the *firsts* – that's what I *mean*, nobody watches Junior Colts B – !

HAPGOOD: I do.

JOE: I *know*, Mum –

HAPGOOD: Well, I won't, then.

JOE: I like you *coming* –

HAPGOOD: I didn't shout this time –

JOE: You did a bit, Mum.

HAPGOOD: Hardly at all, whose boots are those?

JOE: Mine.

HAPGOOD: No, they're not.

JOE: Yes they are, I bought them.

HAPGOOD: Where?

JOE: From Sandilands.

HAPGOOD: Who's Sandilands?

JOE: He's had his kidney out so he does art.

HAPGOOD: Oh. How much?

JOE: A pound.

HAPGOOD: A pound? What was wrong with yours?

JOE: I lost one.

HAPGOOD: You lost a rugby boot?

JOE: Yes. Well, not exactly, I mean I haven't *got* any rugger boots.

HAPGOOD: (*Irked*) Of course you have, what were you playing in before?

JOE: My running shoes – it doesn't matter, nobody minds –

HAPGOOD: You mean you *never* had any rugby boots?

JOE: Only this term, Mother –

HAPGOOD: Why didn't you say? – those look too big anyway, how old is Sandilands?

JOE: It's *all right*, it's silly to buy new boots for Colts B.

HAPGOOD: And now you've lost a running shoe? How did that happen?

JOE: It's not lost, it's on the roof.

HAPGOOD: I don't wish to know about this.

JOE: I borrowed the key for Mr Clark's garage where there's the ladder, I was going to get it down in break with the ladder but then I lost it.

HAPGOOD: The ladder?

JOE: No, *the key*, Mum – I put it somewhere and Mr Clark will have an epi if I don't find it.

HAPGOOD: Is that what you're worried about, Mr Clark's garage key?

BLAIR: I'll send one of the burglars.

JOE: It's all right, don't do anything, Mum –

HAPGOOD: I won't. When was all this?

JOE: Today after breakfast – oh: thank you for the parcel. Your card came too. When were you in Austria? Did you go to the Spanish horses?

HAPGOOD: No. I was too busy. What was in the parcel?

JOE: The chocolate animals.

HAPGOOD: Oh, yes.

JOE: I gave one to Roger.

HAPGOOD: How is Roger?

JOE: I think he's pregnant.

HAPGOOD: Oh dear.

JOE: Well, he's awfully fat and he only eats chocolate.

HAPGOOD: Oh, well . . .

JOE: I've got to go –

HAPGOOD: Yes, don't miss tea – have you told Mr Clark you've lost his garage key?

JOE: No, I mean he doesn't know I borrowed it.

HAPGOOD: Don't tell him yet – do the grid for me. From getting up, to when you couldn't find it. You remember how we do that?

JOE: It's all right, Mother –

HAPGOOD: I know it's all right. Just do the grid – five minutes for every square, don't leave any out because the key is in one of them, and phone me in first break if you haven't found it.

JOE: Yes, all right, thanks, Mum – thanks for coming –

BLAIR: Goodbye, Joe.

JOE: Goodbyes'a.

HAPGOOD: Bye, darling – I'll let you know when I can come again – (*They exchange a kiss and he runs off.*)

BLAIR: (*Suddenly hearty*) I say – what a jolly nice young chap! Excellent knees. You know, you should go to the Spanish Riding School some time when you're next in Vienna – really worth it.

HAPGOOD: (*Tightly*) Right, fine, thanks, point taken – I sent him a postcard; sorry. Oh, sugar, Paul!

BLAIR: I merely said –

HAPGOOD: No, you're right, I break the rules, but I keep *missing* things, last time I missed him in *Robin Hood* even if he *was* only a tree, and if I can't send him a rotten postcard you can take Vienna and stick it up your –

BLAIR: Right, fair enough –

HAPGOOD: – jumper! Oh, fiddle! – I already run the only intelligence network in the Western world which exhibits seasonal fluctuations, and it's only a matter of time before somebody works out it's the school holidays. And now there's Ridley. Really I should pack it in.

BLAIR: Oh, yes, Ridley. You could be right about him. It makes one wonder about that Bulgarian we lost in Paris . . .

HAPGOOD: Ganchev, I thought so too. And Athens.

BLAIR: Yes, Athens. Wates will like that one.

HAPGOOD: It's a mess.

BLAIR: Yes. Frankly I'd rather it were Kerner. That's just a better mousetrap. The real secrets are about intentions and deployment, and Ridley could make it shit city around here, I like the way they talk, the Americans, don't you? – no, of course you don't. What do you say when you burn your hand on a saucepan? 'Oh, sugar'?

HAPGOOD: I don't cook.

BLAIR: I didn't know you knew. Well, what are we going to do about Ridley? We could reel him in for a hostile interview but I'd rather catch him at it.

HAPGOOD: Yes, that's right. We missed our chance today, we'll have to make him do it all again.

BLAIR: (*Surprised*) He won't come back to the well, it's been poisoned.

HAPGOOD: I know. It's difficult. I'll think about it. Do you want some tea? They lay it on for parents and he's entitled to two.

BLAIR: (*Shakes his head*) I think I'd better get the search going in back numbers. Perhaps you could organize a relief team from eight o'clock.

HAPGOOD: I've done that.

BLAIR: And someone should tell Downing Street we're standing by Kerner.

HAPGOOD: I've done that too.

BLAIR: Well . . . (*He nods goodbye at her.*) Don't pack it in yet, I need you.

HAPGOOD: I was calling you at the pool this morning.

BLAIR: I was there.

HAPGOOD: I needed *you*.

BLAIR: No, no, that was only personal. But you're going to need me now.

HAPGOOD: I'll see you tomorrow. I'll be twenty minutes late in, there's something I have to do.

(BLAIR *watches her go. The next time he moves he's in Hapgood's office giving his hat to* MAGGS *and taking off his overcoat.*)

SCENE 4

HAPGOOD's *office, ten a.m.*
There is a door from MAGGS's *office. A window would be nice but is not necessary. There is a desk with the usual stuff including at least two telephones one of which is red. Push-button dialling. You can dial without picking up the receiver, and you can talk to* MAGGS *without*

picking up anything. There is a photograph frame on the desk, not too large. There is a safe. There is a decent old polished table big enough for six people to meet though we never need it for more than four. It might be nice to make the conference table and the desk all one thing so long as HAPGOOD *doesn't look like Mussolini at work. An armchair would be useful but not if it has to be carried on. Anyway, there should be room to walk around.* MAGGS *is Hapgood's secretary. He is young, calm, professional.*

MAGGS: Mrs Hapgood will be late. I've told Mr Wates.
BLAIR: Is he here? I didn't see him.
MAGGS: He's washing his hands and can he have a word.
BLAIR: Well, I'm here.
MAGGS: He said to say he's washing his hands and can he have a word.
BLAIR: Don't be silly.
MAGGS: That's what he said. Can I get you some tea?
BLAIR: No, I don't think so, thank you, I had some. Was that Merryweather out there?
MAGGS: Yes, sir.
BLAIR: Well, somebody should go and tell Mr Wates to stop washing his hands.
MAGGS: I'll ask Mr Merryweather.
(MAGGS *takes* BLAIR's *hat and coat and scarf out. Under the coat* BLAIR *looks a bit rumpled, yesterday's shirt, that sort of feeling. He has a* Daily Telegraph. *He makes himself comfortable and opens it up.*
The red telephone rings. It has its own sound. BLAIR *takes no notice.*
MAGGS *hurries in.*)
BLAIR: It's the red line, I thought I wouldn't get in the way.
MAGGS: (*Into phone*) Mrs Hapgood's office . . . oh, hello, I'm sorry she isn't in . . . Yes, I'm fine, thanks, how are things your end?
(WATES *enters, looking terrific: suit, white shirt, tie, polished shoes. The clothes are loose enough for a gun and the radio to be in there somewhere but not baggy.*
BLAIR *gets up to greet him.*)

BLAIR: Ben! Good morning!

WATES: Paul.

BLAIR: Come in – sit down –

MAGGS: (*Into phone*) . . . Uh, hold on a moment –

BLAIR: Mrs Hapgood won't be long.

MAGGS: (*To* BLAIR) Excuse me – should I . . . ?

BLAIR: No, no – it's perfectly all right.

    (*To* WATES) Downing Street.

WATES: Uh-huh.

MAGGS: (*Into phone, baffled*) You lost Mr Clark's garage key?

BLAIR: (*Hastily*) *The Telegraph* has got a lot better, I notice . . .
    doesn't come off on your hands the way it used to. Maggs
    said you were washing your hands, but he didn't say of what.

WATES: You guys.

BLAIR: (*Cheerfully*) Yes, it's wit city around here.

WATES: No, you're funny like funny money, it doesn't mean
    everything it says.

MAGGS: (*Into phone*) He threw your boot on the roof.

WATES: I'm not listening.

MAGGS: (*Into phone*) Five minutes for every square. Uh-huh. One
    square finding Whitaker for Matron. In the toilet, all right –
    two squares just dossing about, all right –

WATES: What number Downing Street?

MAGGS: (*Into phone*) Oh! Have you got another coin? I'll call you
    straight back from my office.

    (*He puts down the red phone and leaves, closing the door.*)

BLAIR: You wanted a word, I think . . .

WATES: Well . . .

BLAIR: . . . in the washroom.

    (WATES *gets up, or perhaps he hasn't sat down, his manner is
    restless. He picks up the photo on Hapgood's desk.*)

WATES: (*Quietly*) Mother.

BLAIR: Mm?

WATES: Ridley and the other one, Merryweather, they call her
    Mother.

BLAIR: Yes.

WATES: There's a son.

BLAIR: There is a son but she was called Mother when she joined the Defence Liaison Committee – the tea would arrive and the Minister would say, 'Who's going to be mother?'

WATES: She was the only woman.

BLAIR: Yes. She's still the only woman.

WATES: Is there a Mr Hapgood?

BLAIR: No.

WATES: Dead?

BLAIR: Is this idle curiosity?

WATES: You tell me.

BLAIR: Hapgood is her own name. Mrs is a courtesy title. It saves a lot of explanation. Usually.

WATES: Do you mind if I ask you something, Paul?

BLAIR: I'm beginning to.

(WATES *puts the frame carefully back on the desk. Suddenly impatient.*)

WATES: Look, it's simple: do you know who the kid's father is or not?

(BLAIR *stares back at him, quite blank, and* WATES *lets it go.* WATES *has a complaint now.*)

She calls me Wates.

BLAIR: It's a sort of compliment.

WATES: It doesn't sound friendly.

BLAIR: Mister wouldn't be friendly.

WATES: You call me Ben.

BLAIR: That's another sort of compliment.

WATES: She doesn't call me Ben.

BLAIR: That would be friendly but not necessarily a compliment.

WATES: She calls you Paul.

BLAIR: Yes, but we're friends.

WATES: Can you explain this in some way I'd understand it?

(BLAIR *considers the question.*)

BLAIR: No, I don't think so.

WATES: You guys.

BLAIR: What did you want to talk about?

WATES: Ridley.

BLAIR: All right.

WATES: You don't look surprised.

BLAIR: It's deceptive.

WATES: I was thinking about Ridley. Kerner delivers but Ridley intercepts. Ridley intercepts and delivers to Hapgood. Ridley and Hapgood. Hapgood and Ridley. I know the tune. You didn't tell me it was him in Athens.

BLAIR: Oh, yes, Athens.

WATES: Talk to me about Athens, Paul, since we're friends.

BLAIR: Well, we targeted a radio operator in the Russian Embassy in Athens who was cheating on his wife with a local girl we put in his way, a straightforward honeytrap. Mrs Hapgood came out from London to put the squeeze on him. Ridley was at that time number three in the Athens station, he took the photographs. But it went wrong and as you know we had to pull Ridley out of Athens in a hurry.

WATES: He killed an American agent.

BLAIR: That isn't how I'd put it.

WATES: How would you put it?

BLAIR: He killed a Greek national who turned out to be on the Company payroll. Anyway, it was a sideshow. The target's wife found out he was cheating. Next thing, the KGB goons busted our Russian in the girl's flat. Simply bad luck. The girl got roughed up in the process and her pimp took it into his head that Ridley set her up. He tried to shoot Ridley on the stairs of his apartment and Ridley shot him first. Most embarrassing.

WATES: Embarrassing?

BLAIR: For Her Majesty's Government. It nearly cost us the Elgin Marbles.

WATES: Look at the score. One American source dead, one Russian target blown, one honeytrap busted – that's three nothing to them, and Ridley moves on to Paris. (*Pause.*) Now I'm thinking about Ganchev, you remember Ganchev?

BLAIR: Ganchev. I can't quite place him.

WATES: Bulgarian. He was one of your joes, shot dead in Paris. He was your Bulgarian – he got blown – the Bulgarians took him out – boom! – and you can't quite place him.

BLAIR: Oh, yes, Ganchev.

WATES: Right, Miron Ganchev. He was Ridley's joe, wasn't he?

BLAIR: Yes, that's right.

WATES: He was making a meet with Ridley and he was killed in a safe house in the rue Velásquez except it wasn't a safe house any more.

BLAIR: Yes.

WATES: It was Ridley's meet. Two doorkeys, whoever gets there first waits for whoever gets there second. Ridley was second.

BLAIR: I think I can see what you're getting at but unfortunately Ganchev was shot at a range of about nine inches and Ridley was in a taxi in a traffic jam on the wrong side of the river. We went into it.

WATES: No, you don't see. Who says he was in a taxi?
(*Pause.*)

BLAIR: (*Quietly*) Ben, I really wouldn't want you to make an ass of yourself.

WATES: Who says he was in a taxi?

BLAIR: Fuck off.

WATES: It was Hapgood. She was in the taxi too. And you went into it. Did you get the taxi driver? No. You had Ridley's boss.

BLAIR: (*Flares up*) What is this – couldn't you sleep? This is stood on *nothing*: if Ridley did it, Hapgood must have alibi'd him: if Hapgood alibi'd him Ridley must have done it. You've got nothing, Ben, except insomnia.

WATES: That's what it was. Nine p.m. Washington time I'm in Grosvenor Square, going through the whole thing again, I'm thinking about the radio signal in Kerner's briefcase. It gets to the meet, no question. Kerner delivers, Ridley collects, Ridley delivers to Hapgood. The signal goes dead.

BLAIR: It's still insomnia.

WATES: (*Imperturbably*) It's still insomnia and I'm still thinking about Kerner's bleep. It went off the air but what does that mean? Maybe it went off the air, maybe we lost the frequency, maybe it hopped frequencies, maybe there was an override, you know what I mean? I didn't believe any of it, I just wanted to get rid of these things so I could forget the bleep and think about something else. So my guy's radio-finder is sitting on the desk and I put on the phones and I tune it in . . . and, Paul, it was alive. It was transmitting like a bullfrog.

BLAIR: Two o'clock in the morning?

WATES: (*Nods*) I start waking people up. I have a vector on it, I need co-ordinates. By four o'clock I know which street, I know the building, I know which corner of the building, I know how high up the building within eight feet, I mean, shit, I know which *room*. It was coming from this office. The bleep has come back home. It's here.

BLAIR: Why didn't you wake me?

WATES: Where were you sleeping?

    (*Pause*)

BLAIR: Where is she now?

WATES: You're asking me?

BLAIR: (*Snaps*) Yes, I'm asking you.

WATES: Excuse me.

    (*He takes the radio out of his coat.*)

    (*To* RADIO) Wates – who's in the Toyota?

RADIO: Collins, sir.

WATES: Where're you at?

RADIO: Outside. Target is home.

    (WATES *puts the radio back in his pocket.*)

WATES: She just walked in.

BLAIR: Good.

WATES: We should hold back a little, feel this thing out.

BLAIR: Don't worry. Incidentally, where did she go this morning?

WATES: Shopping.

BLAIR: Shopping.

WATES: As I say, it makes sense to hold back, Paul, give her a little room, you understand me?

BLAIR: Of course.

    (*The door opens and* HAPGOOD *enters briskly. She has her shopping with her. There is a Lillywhites' carrier bag and a little Fortnum's bag.*)

HAPGOOD: Good morning! – Paul – Wates –

BLAIR: Good morning! – Guess what – Kerner's bleep came alive in the night, it seems to be coming from your office.

WATES: Aw, shit.

HAPGOOD: Golly, Wates.

WATES: I meant golly.

HAPGOOD: Sit down.

WATES: I've been sitting, I like standing, ma'am.

> (MAGGS *enters. He comes from the outer office with stuff for*
> HAPGOOD's *attention; a wooden tray [shallow box] overflowing*
> *with open letters, memos, etc., and a separate lot of sensitive*
> *material which might even be in a little attaché case or a closable*
> *file. The tray is put on the desk; it's the other lot of stuff which*
> HAPGOOD *looks through first.*)

MAGGS: Good morning. Do you want to see the decrypts?

> (HAPGOOD *is behind her desk.* BLAIR *has sat down again where*
> *he was sitting, and* WATES *probably stays standing.* MAGGS
> *stands.*)

HAPGOOD: (*To* MAGGS) Thank you. Anything else?

MAGGS: Joe telephoned. I wrote down the grid.

HAPGOOD: Thank you – don't go. (*To* WATES) What time, Wates?

WATES: One fifty – two o'clock . . .

HAPGOOD: Uh-huh.

> (*She has scooped the decrypts, etc., out of their case.* MAGGS *gets*
> *the case.* HAPGOOD *starts going through the pile of stuff. There's*
> *not very much of it. But unless otherwise stated she is reading the*
> *material continuously, making notes on pages which one by one*
> *go back to* MAGGS *and back into the case. She reads while she*
> *listens and she also reads while she talks to* WATES. *But for*
> BLAIR *she looks up.*)

> (*To* BLAIR) Did you see this from the Listeners?

BLAIR: Mm. I'll believe it when it happens.

HAPGOOD: (*To* WATES) It was alive when you checked, so you
> don't know when it came on air.

WATES: That's right.

HAPGOOD: (*To* MAGGS) This one to Special Branch in the pouch.
> This one to the Russian Desk by hand.
> (*To* WATES) And you got a triangulation and the beams
> crossed in this office.

WATES: Yes, ma'am.

HAPGOOD: Is it still giving out?

WATES: As far as I know.

HAPGOOD: And you would know, wouldn't you?

> (*It is clear now that he is not popular with her this morning.*)

(*Icy*) Why didn't you call me?

(*He doesn't reply so she gives him a glance.*)

Yes, I see.

(*She bangs a few buttons on her telephone console and then lifts the handset.*)

(*Into phone*) Get me the form on a white Toyota –

WATES: (*Pleading guilty*) Yeah, all right.

HAPGOOD: (*Into phone*) Cancel.

(*She puts the phone down.*)

(*To* WATES) I'll get back to that. So did you bring a radio-finder with you?

(*To* MAGGS) This one upstairs, this one reconfirm.

WATES: No, ma'am.

HAPGOOD: You thought you'd give me first crack. That's all right.

WATES: Ma'am, this is a 500 millisecond-repeat transponder-transmitter locked on seventeen megahertz with a lithium battery and a gate interrupter . . . it . . .

(*He falters because she appears to be absorbed in her next paper.*)

HAPGOOD: Interrupter.

WATES: It gives it a signature, it has to be the same bleep.

(*She scribbles on the last decrypt, hands it to* MAGGS *and takes the top sheet off the other pile.*)

HAPGOOD: So it went dead at ten-oh-seven yesterday morning and it was alive again at two a.m. Can they come and go like that?

WATES: Not that I ever heard. My guy couldn't figure it either. They're either fixed or broke, they don't fix themselves.

HAPGOOD: Uh-huh. Did he mention a hamster?

WATES: A what?

HAPGOOD: (*To* MAGGS) Roger.

MAGGS: No.

HAPGOOD: You sure? – empty square before assembly –

MAGGS: No Roger-the-hamster.

HAPGOOD: Oh, the chump. (*Relieved*) That's all, Maggs. Tea.

(MAGGS *goes back to his office.* WATES *has had enough of this.*)

WATES: Excuse me – we don't need to know about this stuff.

When I put on the phones I felt foolish like putting on a

stethoscope for a corpse that's been ten hours dead in the
water – but, ma'am, we've got a situation now and I'm glad
Paul is here because I'm asking him to ask you if you would
open up that safe you have there and then I won't have to
worry about it any more.

(HAPGOOD *has stopped listening. She sits thinking.*)

Paul?

(*He gets no help.*)

HAPGOOD: Wates, I could kiss you.

(*She goes to the door.*)

Merryweather.

(*She heads back to her desk.*)

MERRYWEATHER: (*Entering*) Thanks, Mother, I don't need long,
it was just that I had a thought about our Russian friend –

HAPGOOD: (*Sitting down*) In a minute. You drained the pool.

MERRYWEATHER: Yes, that's right.

HAPGOOD: How long did that take?

MERRYWEATHER: Ages – most of the day – right down to the
filter –

HAPGOOD: And?

MERRYWEATHER: I put it in Maggs's box last night.

(*He means an envelope on Maggs's pile.* HAPGOOD *tears the
envelope across.*)

Looked interesting to me. Any good?

(*The envelope contains a 'poker chip' transmitter. She tosses it to*
WATES *who catches it.*)

HAPGOOD: Ten hours dead in the water. It only drowns the
signal, when Merryweather fished it out it was back on the
air.

(MAGGS *comes in with* HAPGOOD's *tea. It's like having tea at the
Ritz without the sandwiches – nice china, tea pot, hot water jug,
etc.*

BLAIR, *who has been sitting too still for too long, now stretches
all the tension out of his body, sprawling in his chair, languid
again.*)

BLAIR: I think I might change my mind about that tea, Maggs . . .
how about you, Ben?

WATES: Yes. Thank you.

HAPGOOD: Just the cups, Maggs. Mr Wates takes it with lemon.

MAGGS: We haven't got a lemon.

HAPGOOD: Tsk, tsk, you must always keep a lemon.

MAGGS: (*Leaving*) The reply from Ottawa came in.

HAPGOOD: Oh yes?

MAGGS: Exchange bishops, and queen to king one.

HAPGOOD: Exchange bishops, my eye – he'll be lucky.

> (MAGGS *leaves.* HAPGOOD *broods for a moment. From his pocket,* WATES *produces his pink-paper 'diagram'. He looks at it and passes it to* BLAIR. *Meanwhile –*)

MERRYWEATHER: Mother . . .

HAPGOOD: Oh, I'm sorry, Merryweather –

MERRYWEATHER: It's just that I had a thought which may or may not be something.

HAPGOOD: Of course – tell us your thought.

MERRYWEATHER: Well, I was thinking about it and something wasn't quite right. The Russian delivered to the changing room and he came straight out again . . .

HAPGOOD: Yes?

MERRYWEATHER: He didn't have time for a swim or anything.

HAPGOOD: Uh-huh.

MERRYWEATHER: Well, this is the thing – I was thinking about it and I'm pretty sure his towel was dry when I followed him in but it was wet when I followed him out . . . I was wondering if anybody had noticed that. (*Pause.*) Well, it was just a thought I thought I'd leave with you.

HAPGOOD: It's a good thought, Merryweather, worth thinking about. Thank you.

MERRYWEATHER: Fine. Any way I can help.

HAPGOOD: Actually, there's a job you can do for me.

MERRYWEATHER: Good – of course –

HAPGOOD: It's down the A30 past Staines.

MERRYWEATHER: Right. A meet?

HAPGOOD: A sort of meet. Just past Virginia Water you take a right, the A329 to Bracknell, a couple of miles along there's a prep school, St Christopher's.

> (*From the Lillywhites' bag she produces a pair of brand new rugby boots and gives them to* MERRYWEATHER.)

Get there at exactly one fifty. You'll find a lot of small boys charging around outside. Stop the first boy you see and say, 'Do you know Hapgood?'

MERRYWEATHER: 'Do you know Hapgood?'

HAPGOOD: The boy will say, 'Yes, sir.' There's an outside chance he'll say, 'I am Hapgood, sir,' but probably not. Give him this, and say, 'I have a message from Mother.'

MERRYWEATHER: 'Do you know Hapgood? I have a message from Mother.' Is this the message?

HAPGOOD: No, the message is, 'The garage key is on Roger's hutch.'

MERRYWEATHER: 'The garage key is on Roger's hutch.'
(MAGGS *comes in with the cups. He goes to add them to the tray.*)

HAPGOOD: St Christopher's – the Bracknell road – one fifty.

MERRYWEATHER: Right. 'The garage key is on Roger's hutch.'

HAPGOOD: Thank you very much, Merryweather.
(*She has helped him out of the door.* MAGGS *is following* MERRYWEATHER *out.*)
(*To* MAGGS) Pawn to rook four, and tell him to put his queen back.

MAGGS: (*Continuing out*) Pawn to rook four.
(MAGGS *closes the door behind him. Pause.*)

WATES: It's Ridley.

BLAIR: Mm.

WATES: I'm sorry.
(*He is commiserating, not apologizing.*)
You'll have to turn over everything he ever touched.

HAPGOOD: We're already doing that.

WATES: (*Surprised, wrong-footed*) Since when?

HAPGOOD: Since yesterday. Paul's been here all night.
(*She flicks her thumb along* BLAIR's *jaw bone, a technical gesture.*)
You look awful.
(*That's* WATES *wrong-footed twice.*)
(*To* WATES) Do you remember Ganchev, our Bulgarian? – Paul and I think that's one which needs looking at, did he tell you?

(*That's three times. He is suddenly really angry.*)

WATES: You guys!

HAPGOOD: Wates –

WATES: My friends call me Ben!

HAPGOOD: I don't care what your friends call you, I want to tell
you something – I will not be tagged by your people in my
own *town*! I took them all round Lillywhites and I can
number them off, don't think I can't, I've been followed by
marching bands that did it better, and if they're not pulled
by the time I go to lunch you're off the bus. Is that entirely
clear?

WATES: It's clear.

HAPGOOD: Good. Did they tell you I popped into Fortnum's?
(*From the little Fortnum's bag she takes a lemon, which is all the
bag contains and adds it to the tea-tray.*)
Where are we, Paul?
(BLAIR *passes her* WATES's *pink diagram.*)

BLAIR: Where we are is that when the bleep died it was no longer
in the briefcase, it was in the water, and Ridley was by the
pool. We're no further than that. But it's really quite
attractive: every month, Ridley helps to pack Kerner's
briefcase. That's his job. Kerner's job is handing the
briefcase over to the Russians.

WATES: It's made in heaven.

BLAIR: Yes. The opposition don't care which way Kerner is bent,
either way he's a channel for Ridley. Yesterday it nearly
came apart but only because of the leak in Moscow. Ridley
had to remove the evidence.

WATES: Why did he remove your films?

BLAIR: (*Smoothly*) Obviously because he put *in* a roll of film and
they all look the same.

WATES: And the bleep?

BLAIR: Oh, you know, pass-the-parcel . . . did you ever play that?
The object is not to be the one holding the parcel when the
music stops. Ridley drowned the signal when . . . someone
else was holding the . . .

WATES: (*Deflecting*) Yes, all right. (*Pause.*) And he did all that
without opening the briefcase?

BLAIR: Ah, yes. That's the bit we're still working on.

WATES: I'd say you have a problem.

BLAIR: We have a hypothesis.

WATES: A *hypothesis?*

BLAIR: Mmm. Actually, it's Mr Kerner's hypothesis.

> (BLAIR *and* HAPGOOD *are complicitly wary of* WATES, *not secretive but slightly embarrassed, expecting his derision.*)

WATES: And is this *hypothesis* a hypothesis you can share?

HAPGOOD: It's twins.

WATES: It's twins?

HAPGOOD: Two Ridleys.

> (*Long pause.* BLAIR *and* HAPGOOD *watch him nervously.*)

WATES: (*Evenly*) Yeah . . . that would do it.

> (HAPGOOD *and* BLAIR *relax.*)

HAPGOOD: Thank you, Ben. Well, should I be mother?

SCENE 5

An indoor shooting range. But we don't really know that yet. We see
RIDLEY, *downstage in the only lit area, ready to shoot, holding his*
gun towards the dark upstage. RIDLEY *shoots six times. His shots are*
aimed at six illuminated targets which make their sudden and
successive appearances. Some of the targets are 'blue' and some (most)
are 'green'. (Or, cut-out figures, of villains and civilians, with some
changes to the dialogue.)
No targets are showing when we see RIDLEY. *He starts shooting when*
the first target appears.
RIDLEY'*s six targets come up as four greens, then a blue, then a green.*
He hits the first two, misses the third and fourth, hits the fifth, which is
the blue, and the sixth. RIDLEY'*s conversation is with an amplified*
VOICE. RIDLEY *doesn't have to raise his voice to reply, but his voice*
echoes.

VOICE: Stop shooting. Two misses, three greens and you killed a
blue. Reload.

RIDLEY: Reloading.

VOICE: On your go, and remember blue is our side.

RIDLEY: Yes, sir.

(HAPGOOD *enters quietly, walking behind* RIDLEY's *back.*)

VOICE: Mr Ridley, on your go.

RIDLEY: Go.

(*The first target is blue.* RIDLEY *lets it live. The next five are all green, rapid.* RIDLEY *hits four, misses the fifth, and hardly has time to curse before the target is knocked out by a sixth shot, from* HAPGOOD's *gun.*)

VOICE: Wait a minute – wait a minute –

(HAPGOOD *comes into* RIDLEY's *light, putting a small automatic into her handbag.*)

HAPGOOD: Hey, Ridley.

RIDLEY: Mother.

VOICE: Is that you, Mrs Hapgood?

HAPGOOD: (*Cheerful*) Hello, Mac. How've you been?

VOICE: Ma'am, you're breaking the rules.

HAPGOOD: I know, I'm hopeless. Will you give us the shop for a while?

VOICE: Do you want the mike?

HAPGOOD: No, no need.

VOICE: I'll be in the back.

HAPGOOD: Thank you.

(*We lose the echo.*)

(*To* RIDLEY) I have to talk to you.

RIDLEY: Funny place to choose.

HAPGOOD: I'm not sure that I want to be seen with you, Ridley.

(RIDLEY *considers this. He considers her. He has his gun in his hand. He puts the gun away behind him, into his waistband under his jacket next to his spine. He takes out a packet of cigarettes, puts one in his mouth, puts the packet away, and feels for the lighter.*)

Don't light it.

(RIDLEY *takes the cigarette out of his mouth and holds it unlit.*)

RIDLEY: What's the problem?

HAPGOOD: The problem is, someone's playing dirty and we're favourite.

RIDLEY: (*Quite pleased*) You and me? What have we done?

HAPGOOD: The story is we're bent. We've been using Kerner to

pass real secrets. Yesterday it went wrong for us and we had
to steal them back during the meet. You passed the briefcase
to me and I emptied it.

RIDLEY: If this is Wates why doesn't he go for the obvious? The
stuff was never in there.

HAPGOOD: Wates tracked it to the pool, he had a finder on the
bleep. It stayed alive till the briefcase got to me.
(RIDLEY *laughs*.)

RIDLEY: I think I see. You cracked the transponder in your teeth.

HAPGOOD: I was in the shower. It doesn't work in water.
(RIDLEY *likes that even better*.)

RIDLEY: And what about the Geiger? Weren't you clean?

HAPGOOD: No. When I opened the briefcase to see if we had a
result . . . How do you like it so far?

RIDLEY: (*Delighted*) It's beautiful. I'm beginning to think you did
it. I don't see that you'd need me.

HAPGOOD: Well, there are a couple of other things. Wates has
been digging up the back garden and he thinks he's found
some bones he can make bodies out of.

RIDLEY: Like what?

HAPGOOD: Like Athens.

RIDLEY: Ah, Athens. We *met* in Athens. Oh, Mother . . . Athens
was the best time of my life.

HAPGOOD: Was it? We had an operation that blew up in our faces.

RIDLEY: What's that to Wates?

HAPGOOD: Well, that girl in Athens, the night she was busted,
she said you were there, outside.

RIDLEY: That was rubbish. I was with you.

HAPGOOD: I know.

RIDLEY: In a parked car in Piraeus waiting for our Russian who
never turned up, we were pretending to be lovers.

HAPGOOD: Don't leer, it suits you.

RIDLEY: What else?

HAPGOOD: Ganchev.

RIDLEY: Good heavens. What a team.

HAPGOOD: I tell you, Ridley, I'm sick of being your alibi. I can't
blame Wates for wondering about us.

RIDLEY: Did Wates talk to you?

HAPGOOD: No.

RIDLEY: He talked to Paul Blair? Blair wouldn't be impressed.
It's all circular. It can't be me without you, it can't be you
without me, so it's both of us. Whatever happened to
neither? Did Blair listen?

HAPGOOD: He listened but he thinks he knows better.

RIDLEY: Trust, you see.

HAPGOOD: No, he thinks it's Kerner.

RIDLEY: Yes, that makes sense.

HAPGOOD: Why?

RIDLEY: Every double is a risk – Blair would have to consider it.

HAPGOOD: Well, I hope he's wrong.

RIDLEY: That's a funny thing to say, Mother.

HAPGOOD: (*With passion*) *Kerner is my joe!* I turned him. If he's
bent, something must have turned him back again –
recently, a few months . . .

RIDLEY: What would that be?

HAPGOOD: (*Shrugs*) *Toska po rodine.*

RIDLEY: What's that?

HAPGOOD: Homesickness, but squared. You have to be Russian.

RIDLEY: That could be. Did he leave a family?

HAPGOOD: Why?

RIDLEY: When I processed him after the meet I found a
photograph, fingernail size, cut out with scissors, like from a
team photo. It was hidden in the lining of his wallet, an
amateur job . . . picture of a boy in a football shirt.

HAPGOOD: (*Looks at him steadily*) What did you do with it?

RIDLEY: I put it back, Mother. Do I have to keep calling you
Mother? You can call me Ernest. (*Pause.*) Call me Ridley.

HAPGOOD: You're all right, Ridley. The firm will miss you.

RIDLEY: Say again?

HAPGOOD: You're suspended. So am I. Wates took his story
upstairs. Paul Blair is running my operations. Do you think I
got you here for fun?

RIDLEY: God almighty. What do we do now?

HAPGOOD: You do what Blair tells you. In my office, seven
o'clock, and you're there to listen, don't talk out of turn. By
the way, we're not telling the Americans.

RIDLEY: Trust me. (*Then a flat challenge.*) Why don't you, as a matter of fact?

HAPGOOD: You're not safe, Ridley. You're cocky and I like prudence, you're street smart and this is a boardgame. In Paris you bounced around like Tigger, you thought it was cowboys and Indians. In Athens you killed a man and it was the best time of your life, you thought it was sexy. You're not my type. You're my alibi and I'm yours. Trust doesn't come into it.

RIDLEY: Well, go and fuck yourself, Hapgood, (*he now takes his lighter out and lights his cigarette with deliberate, insolent defiance*) since we're on suspension. You come on like you're running your joes from the senior common room and butter wouldn't melt in your pants but you operate like a circular saw, and you pulled me to watch your back because when this is a street business I'm your bloody type all right, and in Athens if you could have got your bodice up past your brain you would have screwed me and liked it.

(*He starts to leave.*)

HAPGOOD: Ridley.

(*He stops.*)

Safety.

RIDLEY: I didn't reload.

HAPGOOD: You saved on the blue.

RIDLEY: That's true.

(*He takes his gun from the holster, checks it and puts it back.*)

This is all right.

HAPGOOD: What is?

RIDLEY: I like it when it's you and me.

(RIDLEY *leaves.*

KERNER *enters, coming towards her out of the dark and into the light. She sees him and is not surprised. She takes her radio out of her bag.*)

HAPGOOD: (*To* RADIO) Is he clear?

RADIO: Green.

HAPGOOD: I'm here to be told.

(*She puts the radio back into her bag.*)

(*To* KERNER) Do you mean there's another one like him?

KERNER: It's a hypothesis.

HAPGOOD: So where's the other one?

KERNER: Maybe that was the other one.

HAPGOOD: Joseph!

(*Their manner is as of intimate friends.*)

Did you look at Wates's diagram?

KERNER: (*Nods*) Positional geometry. Leibnitz. I'll tell you about
him.

HAPGOOD: No, don't.

KERNER: You're right, it's marginal. I'll tell you about Leonhard
Euler. Were you ever in Kaliningrad?

HAPGOOD: No, I'm afraid not.

KERNER: I was born in Kaliningrad. So was Immanuel Kant, as a
matter of fact. There is quite a nice statue of him. Of course,
it was not Kaliningrad then, it was Konigsberg, seat of the
Archdukes of Prussia. President Truman gave Konigsberg to
Stalin. My parents were not consulted and I missed being
German by a few months. Well, in Immanuel Kant's
Konigsberg there were seven bridges. The river Pregel, now
Pregolya, divides around an island and then divides again,
imagine nutcrackers with one bridge across each of the
handles and one across the hinge and four bridges on to the
island which would be the walnut if you were cracking
walnuts. An ancient amusement of the people of Konigsberg
was to try to cross all seven bridges without crossing any of
them twice. It looked possible but nobody had solved it.
Now, when Kant was ten years old . . . what do you think?

HAPGOOD: Did he really? What a charming story.

KERNER: The little Kant had no idea either. No, when Kant was
ten years old, the Swiss mathematician Leonhard Euler took
up the problem of the seven bridges and he presented his
solution in the form of a general principle. Of course, Euler
didn't waste his time walking around Konigsberg, he only
needed the geometry.

(*He now produces* WATES's *diagram on pink paper*.)

When I looked at Wates's diagram I saw that Euler had
already done the proof. It was the bridges of Konigsberg,
only simpler.

HAPGOOD: What did Euler prove?

KERNER: It can't be done, you need two walkers.

> (*Pause.*)

HAPGOOD: Good old Euler.

KERNER: You like it?

HAPGOOD: (*Nods*) It makes sense of those twin Russians trailing their coats around the pool. Last year the Swedes got themselves a KGB defector and the famous twins turned up in his debriefing with a solid London connection. If two Ridleys are for real they must have felt the draught. Those two jokers at the meet were brought in as decoys. Reflectors. I never believed in the twins till then. I know about reflectors.

KERNER: Has this place been dusted?

HAPGOOD: Dusted?

KERNER: We can talk?

HAPGOOD: (*Amused*) Oh, yes. We can talk. (*She regards him steadily.*) *Now* he's careful.

KERNER: The photograph? I'm ashamed.

HAPGOOD: (*Sudden force*) No, I am. Oh, fiddle!

KERNER: I mean, 'an amateur job'.

HAPGOOD: Oh, Joseph.

KERNER: Yes, I'm one of your Joes. How is the little one?

HAPGOOD: He's all right. He's fine. Stop sending him chocolates, they're bad for his teeth and not good for his hamster. Dusted is fingerprints, you know. Microphones is swept. Where do you pick up these things?

KERNER: Spy stories. I like them. Well, they're different, you know. Not from each other naturally. I read in hope but they all surprise in the same way. Ridley is not very nice: he'll turn out to be all right. Blair will be the traitor: the one you liked. This is how the author says, 'You see! Life is not like books, alas!' They're all like that. I don't mind. I love the language.

HAPGOOD: (*The language lover*) I'm awfully glad.

KERNER: Safe house, sleeper, cover, joe . . . I love it. When I have learned the language I will write my own book. The traitor will be the one you don't like very much, it will be a scandal. Also I will reveal him at the beginning. I don't understand this mania for surprises. If the author knows, it's rude not to tell. In science this is understood: what is interesting is to know what is happening. When I write an experiment I do not wish you to be *surprised*, it is not a *joke*. This is why a science paper is a beautiful thing: first, here is what we will find; now here is how we find it; here is the first puzzle, here is the answer, now we can move on. This is polite. We don't save up all the puzzles to make a triumph for the author.

HAPGOOD: (*Insisting*) *Joseph* – twins. Who's in charge and is he sane?

KERNER: His name was Konstantine Belov, and, yes, he was sane, though in my opinion absurd.

HAPGOOD: More.

KERNER: He is not in charge now. The twins are his legacy.

HAPGOOD: You knew him?

KERNER: Sure. His training was particle physics, before he got into State Security. One day Konstantin Belov jumped out of his bathtub and shouted 'Eureka!' Maybe he was asleep in the bath. The particle world is the dream world of the intelligence officer. An electron can be here or there at the same moment. You can choose. It can go from here to there without going in between; it can pass through two doors at the same time, or from one door to another by a path which is there for all to see until someone looks, and then the act of looking has made it take a different path. Its movements cannot be anticipated because it has no reasons. It defeats surveillance because when you know what it's doing you can't be certain where it is, and when you know where it is you can't be certain what it's doing: Heisenberg's uncertainty principle; and this is not because you're not looking carefully enough, it is because there is *no such thing* as an electron with a definite position and a definite momentum; you fix one, you lose the other, and it's all done without tricks, it's the real world, it is awake.

HAPGOOD: Joseph, please explain to me about the twins.

KERNER: I just did but you missed it.

(*Pause.*)

HAPGOOD: It's crazy.

KERNER: (*Unmoved*) Oh, yes . . . but compared to the electron it is banal . . . Yelizaveta, when things get very small they get truly crazy, and you don't know how small things can be, you think you know but you don't know. I could put an atom into your hand for every second since the world began and you would have to squint to see the dot of atoms in your palm. So now make a fist, and if your fist is as big as the nucleus of one atom then the atom is as big as St Paul's, and if it happens to be a hydrogen atom then it has a single electron flitting about like a moth in the empty cathedral, now by the dome, now by the altar . . . Every atom is a cathedral. I cannot stand the pictures of atoms they put in schoolbooks, like a little solar system: Bohr's atom. Forget it. You can't make a picture of what Bohr proposed, an electron does not go round like a planet, it is like a moth which was there a moment ago, it gains or loses a quantum of energy and it jumps, and at the moment of quantum jump it is like *two* moths, one to be here and one to stop being there; an electron is like twins, each one unique, a unique twin.

HAPGOOD: Its own alibi.

KERNER: It upset Einstein very much, you know, all that damned uncertainty, it spoiled his idea of God, which I tell you frankly is the only idea of Einstein's I never understood. He couldn't believe in a God who threw dice. He should have come to me, I would have told him, 'Listen, Albert, He threw *you* – look around, He never stops.' What is a hamster, by the way? No, tell me in a minute, I want to tell you something first. There is a straight ladder from the atom to the grain of sand, and the only real mystery in physics is the missing rung. Below it, particle physics; above it, classical physics; but in between, metaphysics. All the mystery in life turns out to be this same mystery, the join between things which are distinct and yet continuous, body and mind, free will and causality, living cells and life itself; the moment before the foetus. Who needed God when everything worked like billiard balls? What were you going to say?

HAPGOOD: It's like a fat rabbit with no ears.

KERNER: Oh yes. You mean a *khomyak*.

HAPGOOD: Yes, a *khomyak* called Roger. (*Pause.*) Joseph, after this thing with Ridley you're blown, you know, your career will be over.

KERNER: Except as a scientist, you mean.

HAPGOOD: Yes, that's what I mean, I won't need you any more, I mean I'll need you again – oh, sugar! – you *know* what I mean – do you want to marry me? I think I'd like to be married. Well, don't look like that.

KERNER: What is this? – because of a photograph in my wallet? It is not even necessary, I never look at it.

HAPGOOD: Won't you want to meet him now?

KERNER: Oh, yes. 'This is Joe.' 'Hello, young man.'

HAPGOOD: (*Defiantly*) Well, I'm going to tell him, whether you marry me or not.

KERNER: I'm not charmed by this. If I loved you it was so long ago I had to tell you in Russian and you kept the tape running. It was not a safe house for love. The spy was falling in love with the case-officer, you could hear it on the playback. One day you switched off the hidden microphone and got pregnant.

HAPGOOD: That's uncalled for. I loved you.

KERNER: You interrogated me. Weeks, months, every day. I was your thought, your objective . . . If love was like that it would not even be healthy.

HAPGOOD: (*Stubbornly*) I loved you, Joseph.

KERNER: You fell into your own honeypot –

HAPGOOD: (*Flares*) That's a damned lie! You unspeakable *cad*!

KERNER: – and *now* you think you'd like to be married, and tell Joe he has a father after all, not dead after all, only a secret, we are all in the secret service! – no, I don't think so. And suppose I decided to return.

(*That brings her up short.*)

HAPGOOD: Where? Why would you do that?

KERNER: Toska po rodine.

HAPGOOD: You mustn't say that to me, Joseph. Please don't say it.

42

KERNER: You would not tell.

HAPGOOD: I might. Take it back.

 (KERNER *comforts her.*)

KERNER: Milaya moya, rodnaya moya . . . it's all right. I am your Joe.

 (*She suffers his embrace, then softens into it.*)

 Cad is good. I like cad.

HAPGOOD: Honeypot . . .

KERNER: Is that wrong?

HAPGOOD: Honey*trap*. And anyway that's something else. You and your books.

KERNER: I thought you would marry Paul.

 (*Wrong.* HAPGOOD *stiffens, separates herself.*)

HAPGOOD: I'll see you tonight. And let Paul do the talking. Keep your end of it as simple as you can.

KERNER: Worry about yourself. I will be magnificent.

ACT TWO

SCENE I

HAPGOOD's *office evening.* BLAIR *sits in Hapgood's place.* HAPGOOD *sits to one side.* RIDLEY *sits to the other side. They are waiting. When* RIDLEY *gets bored with this he opens his mouth to say something.*

BLAIR: (*Mildly*) Shut up, Ridley.
> (*The door opens and* MAGGS *comes in with a potted plant, with card attached, and delivers it to* HAPGOOD. *She opens the little envelope and looks at the florist's card, replaces the card and puts the envelope back where it started on the potted plant. Meanwhile* MAGGS *receives a nod from* BLAIR *and leaves the room, returning immediately to let* KERNER *into the room.* MAGGS *retires again closing the door.*)
> (*Greeting* KERNER) Joseph!

KERNER: Hello, Paul.

BLAIR: Sit here, won't you?

KERNER: (*Turns to* HAPGOOD) So. Something special.
> (HAPGOOD *ignores his glance. After a slight pause,* KERNER *takes the chair down-table opposite* BLAIR.)

BLAIR: This is a friendly interview. That's a technical term. It means it is not a hostile interview, which is also a technical term. I'll define them if you wish.
> (*Pause.*) Well, I won't protract this.
> (*From a dossier he produces about half a dozen five-by-eight black and white photographs; pages from a typewritten document.*)
> Have a look at these, would you?
> (*He pushes them down the table to* KERNER *who spreads them face up in front of him.*)
> I'm afraid they're not very good – photographs of photographs – but you can probably see what they are.

KERNER: Of course.

BLAIR: One of your regular reports on the anti-matter programme you're running with the Centre for Nuclear Research in Geneva, April/May; copies to the main contractors, the

Livermore Research Laboratory in California, through the
SDI office in the Pentagon, travelling by embassy courier
from Grosvenor Square; and copies to the Defence Liaison
Committee, also by hand; both lots under the control of this
office, where indeed the copies are made; a very limited
circulation, fifteen copies in all, nine American and six
British. In fact, however, these photographs are of a British
copy. The white patches are the erasure of the circulation
number printed on to each page *ab origine*. Washington adds
an American circulation prefix, missing from these pages but
not erased. All clear so far?

KERNER: Where did the photos come from?

BLAIR: Moscow. They were received in Washington two days ago
from an American agent in place, not an *American*, of course;
'in place' means –

KERNER: Please, I am not illiterate.

BLAIR: The six British copies have a read-and-return distribution
of eleven. That includes the Minister, the Liaison
Committee and the Prime Minister's box. It doesn't include
your lab, or this office where our copy is kept on file with the
turnkeys.

KERNER: May I ask a question?

BLAIR: Yes, do.

KERNER: Why are you sitting in Mrs Hapgood's chair?

BLAIR: That is a very fair question. The answer is that Mrs
Hapgood isn't here. Mr Ridley isn't here either. They are on
paid leave, which is why they can't be with us this evening,
and which is why this is a friendly interview.

KERNER: (*Laughs*) Oh, Paul, have you broken the rules at last? –
turned by a pair of pretty eyelashes?

HAPGOOD: Behave yourself, damn you!

BLAIR: (*Intervenes calmingly*) Please . . . As you know, there is a
regular traffic of monitored information going to the Soviets
from this office, organized and prepared by Mrs Hapgood
and Mr Ridley, and delivered to you for delivery to your
Russian control. In other words a channel already exists. As
a precautionary measure, Mrs Hapgood and Mr Ridley have
been relieved of their duties. In the same spirit of caution

rather than insinuation, your research programme will have to be interrupted for a while, in the national interest. Notice of your own suspension will reach you by messenger at eight o'clock in the morning.

KERNER: Paul, listen – you don't know how many people get their hands on this . . . my lab – the Whitehall secretariat, the turnkeys, the Minister's wife, his mistress – who knows? – also it could be an American Embassy copy before it receives the Washington prefix. There's probably fifty, sixty people, the channel means nothing.

BLAIR: The pages were photographed on some kind of table-top, I expect a little hurriedly as is often the way in these affairs. The last page – photograph number six – is not well framed. You can see how it happens: the pages were pinned together at top left and turned over one by one, and the five turned pages have twisted the sixth page a little askew. The frame has caught the edge of a further document lying underneath. (*He reaches into his dossier again and produces another photograph which he slides down the table.*)
This is the enlargement. It is in fact a set of angular distributions of neutron production on a uranium target in a cyclotron, whatever that may be and I don't want you to tell me. The important point is that taking the two documents together, we are talking about something which has a circulation of three, which is why I thought I'd bring you together for a chat, just between ourselves for a moment. (*He includes* HAPGOOD *and* RIDLEY *who stay expressionless.*)
I'm sorry it's awkward for you and Mrs Hapgood but these things have to be faced.

KERNER: (*Indicating* RIDLEY) What about him? Isn't it awkward for him?

BLAIR: Yes, but not in isolation. For reasons I can go into if you wish. Ridley – Mr Ridley – and Mrs Hapgood are tied together on this one, for better or worse. (*Pause.*) Well, I'll explain, then.

KERNER: No, it is not necessary.
(*He pushes the photographs back towards* BLAIR.)
Not hurried, only careless.

HAPGOOD: (*Just conversation*) Joseph, don't do this. I don't need it. Tell the truth.

KERNER: The truth is what Paul knows it is.

HAPGOOD: (*To* BLAIR) He's lying to you because he thinks it's me.

(BLAIR *waits*. HAPGOOD *starts to lose control of her tone*.)

Oh, wake up, Paul! Why would he?

(*To* KERNER) Why would you? Why would you give away your work?

KERNER: Because it's mine to give. Whose did you think it was? Yours? Who are you? You and Blair? Dog-catchers. And now you think I am your dog – be careful the dog didn't catch you.

HAPGOOD: Don't give me that!

(*To* BLAIR) He's straight, you know damn well he's straight – he's my joe!

KERNER: (*Laughs, not kindly*) Pride. And your certainty is also amusing – you think you have seen to the bottom of things, but there is no bottom. I cannot see it, and you think you are cleverer than me?

HAPGOOD: (*Heatedly*) He's a physics freak and a maverick, the Russians picked him for this because he had a good defector profile and he didn't fool us, he fooled them, he despises the Soviets, he'd never play ball and he has no reason to. *He has no reason* – give me his reason.

KERNER: They found out about Joe.

(*Pause*. HAPGOOD *poleaxed, as it were*. BLAIR *stays level*.)

Sorry.

BLAIR: How?

KERNER: I don't know.

BLAIR: When?

KERNER: More than a year. They came to me and said, 'Well, so you have a child with your British case-officer. OK – congratulations, we were stupid, but now it is time to mend the damage. For the sake of the boy.'

BLAIR: What did they mean by that?

KERNER: What do *you* think, Paul? I didn't ask.

(*To* HAPGOOD) I had to, Lilya.

HAPGOOD: Joseph. All you had to do was tell me.

KERNER: That is naive.

(*To* BLAIR) Not just the normal reports. You should know this.

BLAIR: What else?

KERNER: My programme.

BLAIR: This trap business?

KERNER: They had the trap, they had the laser optics for handling the particles. They couldn't put it together – nobody could put it together because when you cool it to near-absolute zero –

BLAIR: Joseph – get to it.

KERNER: Everything was halted, it was like needing two trains to arrive together on the same line without destroying each other.

BLAIR: So it couldn't be done?

KERNER: Oh, yes. Like many things which are very difficult it turned out to be not so difficult if you have the right thought. These things are not, after all, trains, they travel at nearly the speed of light, and they are very small, so they can do things which are truly crazy. I was fortunate to have the right thought, and now it was possible to make an experiment with my thought. I worked out the programme for this.

BLAIR: Did they know that?

KERNER: No, we are speaking at last summer. June. But last month was the Geneva test and my programme was good. It could not be contained, of course; a good result is the gossip of the scientific world, and it was the end of the dance for me and my Soviet control. They said I had lied, broken the bargain, they said it was an ultimatum now, or they would take my son, and they absolutely would have taken him.

BLAIR: So you gave it to them.

KERNER: Of course.

HAPGOOD: Paul –

BLAIR: I know. Let me.

(*To* KERNER) But the only meet you've had since your Geneva test was yesterday.

KERNER: I mean yesterday. At the pool.

BLAIR: At the pool? How did you deliver?

KERNER: On disc.

BLAIR: But that was a chickenfeed disc – we cleared the printout.

KERNER: No, it was on the boot-tracks.

BLAIR: Explain that.

KERNER: The normal readout was the chickenfeed. There was a key-code for the hidden files.

(HAPGOOD *stands up*.)

BLAIR: (*To* HAPGOOD) Stay calm. (*He presses the intercom*.) Maggs – come in.

KERNER: What is the matter?

(MAGGS *enters from his office*.)

BLAIR: (*Calmly*) Oh, Maggs . . . get Mrs Hapgood's son to the phone, would you? – headmaster, matron, anybody, but fast.

(HAPGOOD *unfreezes*.)

HAPGOOD: I'll call the payphone, his dorm hasn't gone up.

KERNER: It's all right – they don't want him now –

BLAIR: Go, Maggs!

MAGGS: But Joe isn't there, sir . . . Merryweather came back. Joe wasn't in school – he had permission . . . well, Mrs Hapgood sent for him to be picked up, the driver had a letter –

BLAIR: Merryweather?

MAGGS: He came back at about half past three.

(*To* HAPGOOD) I'm sorry . . . I didn't know you'd be out – it's in your box –

HAPGOOD: *Oh, Christ*, Maggs.

BLAIR: (*To* MAGGS) Go and check.

(MAGGS *goes out.* HAPGOOD *has found Merryweather's message in her in-tray. It is in a sealed envelope which she opens*.)

KERNER: But I gave them everything –

BLAIR: I'm afraid not –

KERNER: Yes I did – I delivered –

BLAIR: Stop talking, Joseph – we intercepted your delivery, they never got your disc.

KERNER: You blowed it! You bloody fool!

(RIDLEY *seems to be out of it. He approaches the desk and picks up the photoframe and looks at it for a moment*.)

RIDLEY: (*To himself*) God Almighty.

(BLAIR *goes to the door and opens it.*)

BLAIR: (*Shouts*) Maggs!

HAPGOOD: (*Calmly enough*) He isn't there, Paul.

(*She has been looking at the contents of Merryweather's message.*)

KERNER: (*To* HAPGOOD) They won't hurt him, they'll want to trade.

BLAIR: I know that but we can't trade.

(*To* HAPGOOD) He's not harmed, he's in a safe house with babysitters – you *know* that. They'll find a way to talk to you but it won't even come to that – it's a local initiative and a stupid one, it's going to be stopped from the Moscow end, I promise you, the diplomatic route and no nonsense –

KERNER: (*Loud*) Don't do that – they can't admit to a thing like this.

BLAIR: You're out of it now –

KERNER: You will put them in a corner –

BLAIR: Then they can crawl out of it –

HAPGOOD: For God's sake shut up!

(*It has become a row.*)

RIDLEY: Why don't we just give it to them? What does it matter? Wait for the call and make the trade. If it comes tonight make it tonight, a kid like that, he should be in bed anyway, we can all get some sleep.

Look, what are we talking about? Are we talking about a list of agents in place? Are we talking about blowing the work names? The cover jobs in the Moscow Embassy? Any of those and all right, the boy maybe has to take his chances. But what has Kerner got? (*Derisively*) The solution to the anti-particle trap! Since when was the anti-particle trap a problem?

(*For a moment* BLAIR *wavers. Then –*)

BLAIR: Shut up, Ridley.

(*To* HAPGOOD) I'll take that disc.

RIDLEY: Don't give it to him.

BLAIR: Ridley, you're out of line.

RIDLEY: (*Loses his temper*) Don't tell me I'm out of line, I know about this and you don't know fuck, all you know is to talk Greek. Kerner is supposed to be the one with the brains and he doesn't have enough to know he's pimping fantasies for people with none. There's nothing on that disc except physics and it will stay physics till little Hapgood is a merchant banker. *There is no gadget here. It has no use.* It's the instructions for one go on a billion dollar train set, and that's all it is. Strategic Defense, my arse.

(*To* KERNER) Listen, you tell them the first time I say something which isn't true and I'll stop. Livermore thinks it can make an X-ray laser to knock out a ballistic missile and Kerner's bit of this is a new kind of percussion cap for the bullet: when the bullet is a laser you need a percussion cap like an H-bomb, one bomb per bullet, naturally it destroys the gun as well as the target but what the hell, all right, you trigger the bomb and the X-rays will lase for you, and if you can do it by putting matter together with anti-matter you get a nice clean bang, no fallout, and Kerner gets the Peace Prize. Leave aside that all the particle accelerators on earth produce no more anti-matter in a year than will make a bang like twenty pounds of dynamite. Leave aside that to make the system work up there in the sky you need about fifty million lines of information code and at NASA they can't handle half a million without launch delays and the Russians probably wouldn't wait. Leave everything aside and there's still the problem that Kerner's bullet can't shoot inside the earth's atmosphere. The gun in the sky is no good for anything except ICBMs coming up through the ceiling, and you've got five minutes because after that your target has turned into eighteen warheads hidden in a hundred decoys and a million bits of tinfoil – and *that's* only until the Russians work out the fast-burn booster which will give you a fighting window of sixty seconds. I mean, this is the military application of Kerner's physics if you're looking ten years ahead, minimum. It's a joke. I'd trade it for my cat if I had a cat.

(*To* BLAIR) And you'll blanket this operation and play ransom games with the little bugger – for what? Do you think you won't screw it up?

51

BLAIR: (*To* HAPGOOD *as though it's just the two of them*) There isn't a *choice*. I'm running this and I'm not giving you a choice. You have to trust me.

(*Pause.* HAPGOOD *opens a drawer in her desk, takes out the electronic 'key', opens the safe, removes a disc-box, closes the safe, gives the box to* BLAIR.)

(*Going, to* KERNER) You're with me.

KERNER: Lilya . . .

HAPGOOD: Do everything Paul says.

(KERNER *follows* BLAIR *out, leaving the door open.* HAPGOOD *sits quietly, looking at nothing.* RIDLEY *doesn't quite know what to do with himself.*)

RIDLEY: Sorry.

(*He gets up and moves towards the door.*)

HAPGOOD: Ridley, close the door.

(RIDLEY *closes the door.*)

I gave him the dummy.

RIDLEY: What?

HAPGOOD: I gave him the dummy disc from your briefcase.

RIDLEY: Christ almighty.

HAPGOOD: If you don't like it you'd better say.

RIDLEY: Like it or not we can't do it, we'll never be clear.

HAPGOOD: We're already in front. They made contact – Blair missed it.

RIDLEY: How?

HAPGOOD: (*Taking the card from the potted plant*) Interflora. 'Mum – I'll phone tomorrow, two o'clock.' I thought – it's not Mother's Day.

RIDLEY: Listen – tell Blair. It's no good without him – he'll have the watchers outside your flat before you get home, you'll be babysat like the Queen of England, nothing will reach you, there'll be a tap on your phone and on every line into this building.

HAPGOOD: Except this one (*the red one*). It's the one Joe will tell them, he knows the trip-code. I've always broken the rules.

RIDLEY: And what then? You won't be able to go to the bathroom, let alone a meet.

HAPGOOD: I know all of that.

RIDLEY: That's if Blair isn't sitting here when the call comes in, he'll go where you go.

HAPGOOD: I won't be here. You'll be here.

RIDLEY: Jesus, I can't answer it. It has to be you.

HAPGOOD: It will be me.

RIDLEY: You can't be in two places at once.

HAPGOOD: (*Suddenly out of patience*) I'm not busking, Ridley, I know how to do this, so is it you and me or not?

(*Pause.* RIDLEY *nods.*)

I'll need two or three hours. Have you got a radio?

RIDLEY: Not with me.

(HAPGOOD *takes her radio out of her bag and gives it to him.*)

HAPGOOD: I'll reach you on it: don't try to talk to me on anything else. Don't go home, go to a hotel.

RIDLEY: Mother, I know what to do. (*He goes to leave.*) Will you be all right?

HAPGOOD: (*Nods*) Stay close.

RIDLEY: It's all right, I'm with you.

(*But she spoils it for him.*)

HAPGOOD: That thing's got a two-mile range, stay close.

(RIDLEY *nods and goes, closing the door.*

HAPGOOD *waits. She opens a desk drawer and takes out another radio. She lays the radio on the desk and waits again. The radio must have a blink-light; perhaps we can see it.* HAPGOOD *picks it up.*)

(*To* RADIO) Is he clear?

RADIO: Green.

HAPGOOD: (*To* RADIO) I'm here to be told.

(*She puts the radio back on the desk. She starts dialling on the red telephone.*

MAGGS *enters, wearing a topcoat.*)

MAGGS: Good night, Mrs Hapgood.

HAPGOOD: Good night, Maggs. Thank you.

MAGGS: I won't ask.

HAPGOOD: That's right, Maggs. By the way, I won't be in tomorrow.

MAGGS: I'll hold the fort.

(MAGGS *leaves closing the door.*)

53

HAPGOOD: (*Into phone, brightly*) Hello! Who's that? . . .
Sandilands! Can you tell Hapgood it's his mother? Wait a
minute, aren't you the one who sells boots? . . . no, no, it's
all right – perfectly all right, in fact quite reasonable, I
thought, you can't get much for a pound nowadays . . . *Two
pounds*? . . . But surely . . .? Oh, a pound *each* – well, fair
enough, yes, I can see that . . . Yes, darling, I'll hold on for
him –
(*In the middle of all that* BLAIR *has quietly entered the room and
is collecting the contents of his dossier, sorting things out, putting
them away.*)
(*Mutters*) Merchant banker . . .?

BLAIR: You know, you're going to get into such trouble one day
. . . I *mean, that's the Downing Street one-to-one red line* – what
are they supposed to think when they pick it up and it's *busy*?

HAPGOOD: Oh God, so it is. (*Huffily*) It's a perfectly natural
mistake, Joe uses it far more than they do.

BLAIR: That's my point. (*Grumbling*) You use the security link
with Ottawa to play chess, you arrive in Vienna after dog-
legging through Amsterdam on a false passport and then
proceed to send postcards home as if you're on bloody
holiday, you use an intelligence officer on government time
to dispatch football boots around the country . . . For
someone who's so safe you're incredibly, I don't know,
there's a little anarchist inside you, I wish you wouldn't . . .

HAPGOOD: Don't be cross, I'm tired.
(*Into phone*) Oh – thank you, Sandilands – I'll hang on,
Paul . . .

BLAIR: Mm?

HAPGOOD: I know this isn't necessary and don't start getting
cross again, I –

BLAIR: (*Somehow irritated, apparently*) It's all right, it's done –

HAPGOOD: You don't know what I –

BLAIR: Yes, yes, watchers at the school till this thing is over, and
Cotton has joined the ground-staff, marking out the rugger
pitches, do him good, he was looking a bit pasty.

HAPGOOD: I absolutely refuse to live without you, do you
understand that?

BLAIR: Of course.

You know, it's going to be tricky doing the swap without a boy to swap.

HAPGOOD: Well, we'll just have to do the best we can, won't we?

BLAIR: Of course.

HAPGOOD: (*Into phone*) Oh, hello, Joe! Are you all right, darling?

(KERNER *enters with a bottle of vodka and three cups.*)

KERNER: Magnificent.

BLAIR: Thank you.

KERNER: No, me. You were terrible. I never believed a word of it.

HAPGOOD: (*Into phone*) No, it was just to tell you not to phone tomorrow in case you were going to. I'm away.

BLAIR: (*To* KERNER) Not even the photographs?

HAPGOOD: (*Into phone*) Oh, good.

KERNER: The photographs I liked.

BLAIR: Yes?

HAPGOOD: (*Into phone*) *In* the hutch? Well, I was nearly right.

(*Meanwhile* KERNER *has poured three tots of vodka into the cups.*)

Thank you, Joseph.

(KERNER *and* BLAIR *toast each other and knock back the vodka.*)

(*Into phone*) Well, you're daft – do they fit? . . .

BLAIR: (*To* KERNER) Come on, then.

(BLAIR *puts his cup down and leaves the room.* KERNER *closes the door after him and remains in the room.*)

HAPGOOD: (*Into phone*) That's all right . . . when is Saturday? The day after tomorrow . . . well, probably, I might. Home or away?

(KERNER *gently takes the phone from her and listens to the phone for a few moments and then gives it back to her, and leaves the room.*)

(*Into phone*) Yes, I'm here. Yes, all right. Well, let me know on Saturday morning.

Yes, Joe, I'm here to be told.

(*She puts the phone down.*)

Now we are in a new place. The first and obvious thing about it is that it is a photographer's studio. The second thing is that it is also where somebody lives; the room is skimpily furnished as a living room. There is a front door and also another closeable door leading to the other rooms in what is evidently the photographer's flat. There is a telephone.

It is mid-morning. The room is empty. The doorbell rings. HAPGOOD *comes flying out from the other door. We haven't seen her like this. She is as different from her other self as the flat is different from her office; the office being rather cleaner, tidier and better organized.* HAPGOOD *opens the front door, and it's* RIDLEY. RIDLEY *has been shopping: glossy Bond Street carrier bags. He stares at her.*

RIDLEY: Mrs Newton?

HAPGOOD: (*Casually*) Oh, shit.

RIDLEY: I'm Ernest.

HAPGOOD: Well, you're not what I want, so keep your clothes on. Stupid bugger! Not you, darling, come in anyway.

(*She is already heading for the telephone.*)

What did they do? Pick you from the catalogue? I'll try and sort it out – charge them for half a day if it looks like their fault – it won't be the first time – (*Now into the phone*) It's Celia, I want Fred.

Would you mind not wandering around.

(*Her last remark needs explaining.* RIDLEY *has dropped his parcels and is now, frankly, casing the joint. He is not taking a lot of notice of her. He moves around coolly as if he owns the place, and in due course he leaves the room, disappearing through the 'kitchen door'.*)

(*Into phone*) Hello, darling, you're losing your grip – I said a Roman soldier, not an Italian waiter, and also he looks queer to me . . . Don't tell me what I mean, you're gay, he's queer, he's got a queer look about him, he won't sell bamboo shoots to a fucking panda, never mind boxer shorts . . . Well, I'll look at his body and let you know – Fred? – Have you gone? – No, the phone clicked –

(*She looks around and finds that the room is empty.*)

Hey – ? What's his name? (*She calls out*) Victor!

(RIDLEY *wanders back into the room.*)

RIDLEY: (*Casual*) Hang up.

HAPGOOD: What do you think you're doing?

(*Into phone*) Is he a regular? Well, I don't fancy him –

(*That's as far as the phone call gets because* RIDLEY, *still maintaining a sort of thoughtful cruise, disconnects the call.*)

Now listen –

(*He looks at her. She goes from fear to relief.*)

You're Betty's friend. God, I am sorry, darling, I'm Celia, don't be offended, being rude about the models is the house style, it saves a lot of nonsense about being paid for the reshoot. And anyway you do look like an Italian waiter. What does Betty want? – I don't owe her any favours, she never does me any, I mean there must be lots of photographic work going in the spy racket. She says I won't keep my mouth shut – can you believe it? Can you smell burning? – Oh, sod!

(*She leaves the room in a hurry.* RIDLEY *has been looking at her like somebody looking at a picture in a gallery. He reaches into his jacket and produces his radio.*)

RIDLEY: (*On* RADIO) Mother.

HAPGOOD: (*On* RADIO) Ridley.

RIDLEY: You're out of your fucking mind.

HAPGOOD: (*On* RADIO) What's the matter?

RIDLEY: She may be your twin but there the resemblance ends. She's a pot-head, it reeks, she's growing the stuff in the window-box, she won't stop talking, she picks her nose, she looks like shit, I mean it doesn't *begin* . . .

HAPGOOD: (*On* RADIO) Where is she?

RIDLEY: In the kitchen burning things . . .

HAPGOOD: (*On* RADIO) I'm signing off.

RIDLEY: No, listen –

(*But evidently she has cut him off. He puts his radio away and goes to pick up his shopping. He puts it on the sofa, perhaps and anyway, starts unloading the carrier bags. They are full of clothes in tissue paper. There's also a shoe box and other stuff. It all adds up to one outfit, suitable for the office.*)

While he is doing this HAPGOOD *bangs her way back into the
room [she probably wouldn't have bothered to close the door so a
door on a spring might be useful].*

*She is nibbling the unburned portion of a croissant, which
rapidly gets as far as the wastepaper basket.*)

HAPGOOD: And you made me warm my croissant to a frazzle. What
have you got there?

RIDLEY: Clothes, shoes, make-up . . . Is there a bathroom?

HAPGOOD: No, we pee in the sink. Can you try to show a little
charm?

RIDLEY: Your sister said do what he tells you.

HAPGOOD: So what?

RIDLEY: Run a bath.

HAPGOOD: Why?

RIDLEY: You look as if you need one.

HAPGOOD: Now just a minute –

RIDLEY: And wash your hair.

HAPGOOD: *Just a minute.* I'm not going to a party, I've got a busy
morning.

RIDLEY: Victor isn't coming. It's ten twenty and we're leaving here
at one fifteen, just under three hours. I'll explain as you go.

HAPGOOD: Will you indeed.

(*She picks up the phone again and starts dialling.*)

RIDLEY: Who are you calling?

HAPGOOD: I want to talk to Betty.

(*Without hurrying much, because she is still dialling,* RIDLEY
*yanks the phone cord which comes away from the wall bringing
fragments of plastic and bits of skirting-board with it.*)

RIDLEY: You don't talk to Betty, you don't talk to anybody, in fact
you don't talk so much in general, and you don't swear at all,
get used to it, please.

HAPGOOD: You bloody gangster, that telephone is my livelihood!

RIDLEY: Is that right? You'll have to fall back on photography.

(*She swings at him. He catches her wrist. With his other hand he
takes a wad of bank notes out of one pocket.*)

That's two thousand pounds.

(*He lets go of her wrist and takes a similar wad out of another
pocket.*)

So's this. That's now, this is later.

HAPGOOD: What is it for?

RIDLEY: It's for looking nice and not talking dirty, and answering a telephone. After that, we'll see.

HAPGOOD: Why?

RIDLEY: I'll tell you when it's time.

HAPGOOD: Then why would I do it?

RIDLEY: For the money, your sister said. I want to know about you and your sister, sibling bribery is a new one on me.

HAPGOOD: Well, you can go and –

RIDLEY: Every time you swear I'm taking £50 out of this bundle. You'll get what's left.

HAPGOOD: – fuck yourself.

(RIDLEY *separates a £50 note from the bundle of money [which is perhaps secured by a rubberband], and puts the remainder back into his pocket.*)

That's theft.

RIDLEY: No, it's arson.

(*Because his hand has come out of his pocket with his cigarette lighter with which he sets fire to the note.*)

HAPGOOD: You're all nutters. I knew it then. Is Betty in trouble?

RIDLEY: When?

HAPGOOD: If she's in trouble, I don't mind helping.

RIDLEY: You knew it when?

HAPGOOD: Whenever – all those years ago when we did the interviews.

RIDLEY: Tell me about that.

HAPGOOD: I failed the attitude test. Betty was exactly their cup of tea so they kept her anyway.

RIDLEY: Anyway?

HAPGOOD: They were seeing twins – it was a phase. Nutters is not the word. (RIDLEY *laughs.*) Ask Betty, they had a reason, she'll know what it was. Well, that cheered you up.

RIDLEY: Yes. Will you have a bath and talk nice and do what I tell you?

HAPGOOD: Is it her money?

RIDLEY: Not exactly.

HAPGOOD: I wouldn't take it if it was hers.

RIDLEY: Fine. It's ten twenty-five.

HAPGOOD: What did you say your name was?

RIDLEY: Ernest. Do you want me to scrub your back?

HAPGOOD: No, thank you.

RIDLEY: Take the clothes. They're for you to put on.

(She gathers them up to take them out.)

HAPGOOD: They're not really me.

RIDLEY: That's right.

(HAPGOOD leaves the room. RIDLEY stays where he is. The next time he moves, he's somebody else.)

INTER-SCENE

So we lose the last set without losing RIDLEY. *When the set has gone,* RIDLEY *is in some other place . . . which may be a railway station, or alternatively a place where boats come in, or an airport; whatever the design will take, really. The main thing is that he is a man arriving somewhere. He carries a suitcase. He is a different* RIDLEY. *It's like a quantum jump.*

And now we lose him. Perhaps he walks out. Perhaps the scene change has been continuous and he is now erased by its completion.

SCENE 3

BLAIR *and* KERNER *are at the zoo.* BLAIR *has the 'pink diagram'.*

BLAIR: I must confess I always thought that one Ridley was enough and occasionally surplus to an ideal arrangement of the universe. Now we've got one in Kensington and one who could be anywhere. I imagine he doesn't hang around, he'd come in and out as required. Could be on a British passport, more likely not. This is, of course, assuming that he exists. Does this *(the diagram)* prove twins?

KERNER: No. An invisible man is also a correct solution.

BLAIR: You chaps.

KERNER: Mathematics does not take pictures of the world, it's only a way of making sense. Twins, waves, black holes – we make bets on what makes best sense. In Athens, in Paris and at the Pool, two Ridleys satisfy the conditions. He was his own alibi. So we're betting on twins. But we need to be lucky also, and today is Friday; is it the thirteenth?

BLAIR: You chaps don't believe in that.

KERNER: Oh, we chaps! Niels Bohr lived in a house with a horseshoe on the wall. When people cried, for God's sake Niels, surely *you* don't believe a horseshoe brings you luck!, he said, no, of course not, but I'm told it works even if you don't believe it.

(BLAIR *continues to look grave.*)

What is the matter, Paul?

BLAIR: Those photographs. Think of Ridley sitting there. He's been sending film to Moscow and now here are these prints, spread out on the table, courtesy of the Washington pouch. Awkward moment for him. And yet, suddenly he's in the clear. Kerner owns up. Well, we can't have Ridley sitting there wondering why you're owning up to his pictures. Ridley knew this wasn't his batch, because he photographed his pages flat, separately; they weren't pinned together by the corners and turned over. And those figures peeping out underneath, the whatsit production in the cyclone-whatever, they were nothing to do with him.

KERNER: I assumed naturally they were not Ridley's pictures.

BLAIR: Did you? I wish you'd said so. I wish you'd said, 'Paul where did you get that photo?' . . . because you see, those cycleclip numbers were pulled together from different sets, the way somebody might do it at the Moscow end, and it really upsets me, Joseph, that you weren't . . . I don't know . . . surprised.

KERNER: Cyclotron, Paul. It's a sensible word. Cycleclip is bizarre by comparison.

(*Pause.*)

Poor Paul. Everybody is a suspect. (*Reminded*) Explain something to me. I forgot to ask Elizabeth. Prime suspect: it's in nearly all the books. I don't understand. A prime is a number which won't divide nicely, and all the suspects are prime. It's the last thing to expect with a suspect. You must look for *squares*. The product of twin roots. Four, nine, sixteen . . . what is the square root of sixteen?

BLAIR: Is this a trick question?

KERNER: For you, probably.

BLAIR: Four, then.

KERNER: Correct. But also minus four. Two correct answers. Positive and negative. (*Pause.*) I'm not going to help you, you know. Yes – no, either – or . . . You have been too long in the spy business, you think everybody has no secret or one big secret, they are what they seem or they are the opposite. You look at me and think: *Which is he?* Plus or minus? If only you could figure it out like looking into me to find my root. And then you still wouldn't know. We're all doubles. Even you. Your cover is Bachelor of Arts first class, with an amusing incomprehension of the sciences, but you insist on laboratory standards for reality, while I insist on its artfulness. So it is with us all, we're not so one-or-the-other. The one who puts on the clothes in the morning is the working majority, but at night – perhaps in the moment before unconsciousness – we meet our sleeper – the priest is visited by the doubter, the Marxist sees the civilizing force of the bourgeoise, the captain of industry admits the justice of common ownership.

BLAIR: And you – what do you admit?

KERNER: My estrangement.

BLAIR: I'm sorry.

KERNER: I'm thinking of going home, perhaps you know.

BLAIR: No, I didn't.

KERNER: Ah, well.

BLAIR: It may be tricky for you.

KERNER: Do you mean leaving or arriving?

BLAIR: That's roughly what I'm asking *you*?

KERNER: Of course. Dog or dog-catcher. I forget. It's true that when the KGB came to me in Kaliningrad I had already thought of coming West, but to be honest the system I hated was the vacuum tube logic system. We were using computers which you had in museums. I wasn't seeking asylum, I was seeking an IBM 195.

BLAIR: No. They put you up to it and Elizabeth turned you. You were her joe.

KERNER: Yes, I was. There is something terrible about love. It uses up all one's moral judgement. Afterwards it is like returning to a system of values, or at least to the attempt.

BLAIR: (*Angrily*) Yes, values. It's not all bloody computers, is it?

KERNER: No. The West is morally superior, in my opinion. It is unjust and corrupt like the East, of course, but here it means the system has failed; at home it means the system is working. But the system can change.

BLAIR: No, it can't. Come on, Joseph, *you know them* – Budapest in '56 – Prague in '68 – Poland in '81 – we've been there! – and it's not going to be different in East Berlin in '89. They can't afford to lose.

KERNER: (*Shrugs*) It's not my job to change it. My friend Georgi has offered to arrange things if I want to go.

BLAIR: Why are you telling me?

KERNER: I declined his offer.

BLAIR: I'm glad, Joseph.

KERNER: I prefer British Airways.
   (*Pause.*)

BLAIR: You should have accepted.

KERNER: (*Angrily*) Oh, yes! – You don't want to look, and then you'll get spy pattern.

BLAIR: I like to know what's what.

KERNER: Of course! Yes – no, either – or.

BLAIR: That's right. You're this or you're that, and you know which. Prophecy is a pastime I can't afford, I've got one of my people working the inside lane on false papers and if she's been set up I'll feed you to the crocodiles.

KERNER: One of your *people*? Oh, Paul. *You* would betray her before I would. My mamushka.

BLAIR: Good. Good, Joseph.
   (*He seems pleased by the way that went.*)
   Now. Is the sister thing going to work?

KERNER: Oh, yes. I was afraid of it, but with Mr Ridley it will be all right.
   (*He starts to leave, pause.*)

63

I never saw Elizabeth sleeping. Interrogation hours, you
know. She said, 'I want to *sleep* with you.' But she never did.
And when I learned to read English books I realized that she
never said it, either.
(KERNER *walks away*.)

HAPGOOD's *office. It's empty.*
The door is opened with a key from the outside. RIDLEY *enters the*
office.

RIDLEY: (*Addressing* HAPGOOD *outside*). Move.
    (HAPGOOD *enters behind him. She is wearing the clothes which he*
    brought to the flat.
    RIDLEY *closes the door.* HAPGOOD *looks around.*
    RIDLEY *has a bag, perhaps a sports holdall.*)
    Sit there.
    (RIDLEY *does everything smoothly and quickly. He riffles through*
    a stack of printed documents [*technical magazines perhaps*] *on the*
    desk and extracts a sealed envelope, which he tears open. It
    contains a small key and a scribble.)
HAPGOOD: What if somebody comes in?
RIDLEY: It's your office, for God's sake.
    (*He gives her the key.*)
    Middle drawer.
    (HAPGOOD *uses the key to open the middle drawer of the desk.*)
    Remote key.
HAPGOOD: This?
    (*She shows him the electronic key for the safe.* RIDLEY *takes it. He*
    consults the scribble, programmes the key, opens the safe. From the
    safe he takes a disc-box – a new one, i.e. a sealed once-only box of
    the same type. He closes the safe. He puts the disc-box into his bag,
    together with the torn envelope and the scribble. During this:)
    Are you going to tell me what I'm doing here?
RIDLEY: Sure. Any phone that rings, don't pick it up. I'll pick it
    up.

(He picks up the red telephone, looks at its underneath, puts it down again; from the bag he takes a simple 'eavesdrop' connection, a single ear-piece ready to be wired up into a telephone receiver; and a screwdriver.

At that moment, the door opens and MAGGS *walks in, with a file, much as yesterday.)*

MAGGS: Good afternoon Mrs Hapgood, you came in after all. Do you want to see the decrypts?

(HAPGOOD *looks at* RIDLEY.)

RIDLEY: Hello, Maggs . . . aren't you supposed to be having lunch?

MAGGS: Yes, sir.

RIDLEY: Well, piss off then. Go to the pub.

MAGGS: I was in the pub. (*To* HAPGOOD) I got the desk to bleep me if you came in – just the top one, really, it's green-routed and Sydney's been on twice this morning.

HAPGOOD: Has he?

MAGGS: Sydney – they only want a yes or no.

RIDLEY: Let them wait.

HAPGOOD: No, I can do that.

RIDLEY: Are you sure, Mother?

HAPGOOD: What's the matter with you today, Ridley?

(HAPGOOD *takes the 'top one' from* MAGGS *and peruses it with interest.*)

Mm . . .

RIDLEY: Perhaps you'd like me to . . .

HAPGOOD: Fascinating.

MAGGS: Just a yes or no.

HAPGOOD: Yes! Definitely yes!

(*She passes the paper smartly back to* MAGGS.)

Thank you, Maggs. I'll do the rest later.

MAGGS: McPherson came in if you want it.

HAPGOOD: Really?

RIDLEY: It's five minutes to two, Mother.

HAPGOOD: I want to know about McPherson.

MAGGS: Bishop to queen two.

(*Pause.*)

HAPGOOD: Right.

RIDLEY: *Mother.*

> (*The red phone rings.* MAGGS *lifts it up.*)

MAGGS: (*To phone*) Mrs Hapgood's office . . . just a moment.

> (*He gives the phone to* HAPGOOD *and leaves.*)

RIDLEY: Shit!

HAPGOOD: What do I do?

RIDLEY: Talk!

> (RIDLEY *has two desperate concerns: to wire up his 'eavesdrop'*
> *and to prompt* HAPGOOD. *But it's hopeless, a mess.*)

HAPGOOD: (*To phone*) Hello . . . yes, it's her, it's me . . .

RIDLEY: '*I want to talk to Joe*' . . . '*I want to talk to Joe!*'

HAPGOOD: (*Covering the phone*) I can't hear! (*Into phone*) Yes . . .
Eleven thirty . . . (*To* RIDLEY) Someone wants a meeting.

RIDLEY: Where? Keep them talking, ask for Joe . . .

HAPGOOD: Yes . . . Where? . . . Right . . .

> (RIDLEY *is nowhere near ready when she puts the phone down.*)

RIDLEY: I'll kill you for this! – Eleven thirty where? *Where?*

> (HAPGOOD *is still contemplating the phone warily.*)

HAPGOOD: Ten Downing Street.

RIDLEY: *What?* Oh, Jesus!

HAPGOOD: Was that it?

RIDLEY: No. I thought they were early.

HAPGOOD: Who's Joe?

> (RIDLEY *ignores her, he works on the red phone.*)

Listen, I can't do this if you don't tell me what I'm doing.

RIDLEY: I'll tell you when it's time to tell you. God almighty . . . I
ought to slap you bow-legged.

HAPGOOD: You don't mean Betty's Joe, do you? Ernie?

RIDLEY: Ridley.

HAPGOOD: Ridley. What's the silly cow been up to?

RIDLEY: Don't you like her?

HAPGOOD: Of course I like her, she's my sister.

> (RIDLEY *completes his work, and pauses to consider her. He's*
> *unsettled, somehow thrown by seeing her in this office, in these*
> *clothes . . . She is so obviously* HAPGOOD.)

RIDLEY: Mrs Newton. What happened to *him?* You're divorced?

HAPGOOD: I'll say. Bastard owes me thousands. Actually it was
Mr Newton who did for Betty and me. She said he'd go bad,

warned me off, sister to sister. So I crossed her off my list
and married him. Then he went bad. So of course I never
forgave her.

Do you mean she plays chess without a board?

RIDLEY: Looks like it.

HAPGOOD: That sounds like her.

RIDLEY: She's something.

HAPGOOD: Showing off, I meant.

RIDLEY: Why aren't you close?

HAPGOOD: Well, she was always the scholarship girl and I was the
delinquent. Having the kid was good for her, she always
thought the delinquents had the bastards and the scholarship
girls had the wedding. It shook up her view of the world,
slightly. Do you mind if I light up?

RIDLEY: She doesn't smoke.

HAPGOOD: It's all right, it's not a real cigarette.

(*She puts a home-made cigarette in her mouth;* RIDLEY *snatches
it away and keeps it.*)

RIDLEY: For God's sake, don't you know where you are?

HAPGOOD: So what do we do now?

RIDLEY: (*Looking at his watch*) We wait.

(*He leans over to reach the buttons on Hapgood's desk.*)
When I do this (*he snaps his fingers*), you say, 'No calls,
Maggs, no interruptions.'

(*He snaps his fingers.*)

HAPGOOD: No calls, Maggs, no interruptions.

MAGGS'S VOICE: Yes, ma'am.

(*Satisfied for the moment, but nervy,* RIDLEY *paces.*)

HAPGOOD: He probably thinks . . .

RIDLEY: Yeh, nice thought.

HAPGOOD: Speak for yourself.

RIDLEY: I was.

HAPGOOD: Don't fancy your fuckin' chances.

(*Pacing,* RIDLEY, *as though absentmindedly, takes the bundle of
money out of his pocket, detaches a £50 note and sets fire to it with
his lighter. He carries on pacing, she carries on looking at him.*)
Sit down, for God's sake.

(RIDLEY *sits at the table.*)

67

Ten of hearts.

RIDLEY: What about it?

HAPGOOD: Ten of hearts – now you.

(RIDLEY *sighs*.)

RIDLEY: King of hearts.

HAPGOOD: Two of clubs.

RIDLEY: Well, what are we playing?

HAPGOOD: Go on.

RIDLEY: Ace of spades.

HAPGOOD: Seven of diamonds.

RIDLEY: Haven't you got any spades?

HAPGOOD: Play your cards.

RIDLEY: Six of hearts.

HAPGOOD: Two of hearts.

RIDLEY: This is stupid. Nine of clubs.

HAPGOOD: Jack of clubs.

RIDLEY: Jack of spades.

HAPGOOD: Snap!! Bad luck . . .

(RIDLEY *jumps irritatedly to his feet, and then the red phone rings*.)

RIDLEY: *Leave it!*

Listen – Betty's Joe has been kidnapped – this is the people who took him.

(*He takes her left hand, calmly, lays it palm-down on the desk, and using his own hand as a blade he chops her hand across the knuckles, with coolly judged force, enough to make her cry out with pain*.)

You want to talk to Joe – where's Joe, where's Joe?

(*He lifts the red phone now and puts it into her right hand, meanwhile putting the extra earpiece in his ear.* HAPGOOD *is whimpering and disoriented*.)

HAPGOOD: (*Into phone*) Hello, where's Joe, I want to talk to Joe –
I – Yes – yes – yes –

Yes. I heard – can I talk to –

(RIDLEY *relaxes. He takes the phone from her gently and replaces it. The phone call has taken perhaps fifteen seconds.* HAPGOOD *springs away from the desk, from him, crying, comforting her injured hand*.)

RIDLEY: You were very good!

HAPGOOD: You bloody maniac!

>(RIDLEY *is disconnecting his eavesdrop, replacing everything into his bag.*)

>Where's Betty? – is it true about Joe?

RIDLEY: Yes, it's true. But we'll get him back. Eight hours to kill.

>(RIDLEY *retrieves her cigarette from his pocket, lights it and puts it in her mouth.*

>HAPGOOD *draws on the cigarette, still shocked, trembling, settling down.*)

>You were fine. We can go now. Me first. Count twelve and I'll see you outside.

>(RIDLEY *picks up his bag. Carefully he takes away her cigarette, takes a drag himself, and keeps the cigarette. He opens the door.*)

>Welcome to the firm.

>(RIDLEY *leaves.*

>   *Left alone,* HAPGOOD *relaxes, although her hand is still painful.* MAGGS *enters anxious.*)

MAGGS: Is everything all right, Mrs Hapgood?

HAPGOOD: Yes, Maggs – everything's fine.

>(*She heads through the open door.*)

>Queen to king one.

MAGGS: (*Following her out*) Queen to king one.

SCENE 5

A cheap hotel room. It is evening; dark. Perhaps a neon sign outside.
HAPGOOD, fully dressed, has gone to sleep on the bed. RIDLEY *stands*
watching her. Perhaps he is changing into the clothes which he will
wear in the next scene.
RIDLEY takes out his radio.

RIDLEY: (*To* RADIO) Mother.

>(*No answer.*)

>(*To* RADIO) Mother.

>(*No answer.*)

(*Louder to* RADIO) Mother – where the hell are you!

(HAPGOOD, *on the bed has stirred awake.*)

HAPGOOD: How much longer?

RIDLEY: A couple of hours.

(*He puts his radio away and takes his gun out of his holster and checks it.*)

HAPGOOD: Ernest . . . I hardly dare ask you this, but is your mother in the secret service too?

(RIDLEY *ignores that. He puts his gun back into the holster.*) What's that for, Ernie?

RIDLEY: It's for killing people. It's a gun.

HAPGOOD: Do you kill people, Ernie?

RIDLEY: You'll be the second.

HAPGOOD: I don't like this.

RIDLEY: Me neither. Somebody's lying to somebody. They're lying to her or she's lying to me.

HAPGOOD: Would she lie to you, Ernie?

RIDLEY: Telling lies is Betty's habit, sweetheart – lies, fraud, entrapment, blackmail, sometimes people die, so Betty can know something which the opposition thinks she doesn't know, most of which doesn't matter a fuck, and that's just the half they didn't *plant* on her – so she's lucky if she comes out better than even, that's the edge she's in it for, and if she's thinking now it wasn't worth one sleepless night for her little prep-school boy, good for her, she had it coming.

HAPGOOD: Maybe she did.

RIDLEY: She should have given him a daddy instead of getting her buzz out of running joes to please an old bastard who . . . (*a thought strikes him, strikes him as funny*) who's been running *her* for years!

HAPGOOD: What do you mean, Ernest?

RIDLEY: Your sister carries a torch. When it came to a choice she traded in a daddy for a joe who would have been blown overnight if he was known to be the father.

HAPGOOD: *Talk English!*

RIDLEY: I'll get her kid back for her but it's only personal. If she's set me up I'll kill her.

HAPGOOD: You're potty about her, Ernest. I'm disappointed in

70

you. You don't know if you're carrying a torch for her or a gun, no wonder you're confused. You're out on a limb for a boy she put there, while she was making the world safe for him to talk properly in and play the game. What a pal, I should have a friend like you.

RIDLEY: It's not her fault. Do you think you cracked it taking snaps of fancy junk? She's all right. Anyway, I like kids, and you never know, now and again someone is telling the truth.

HAPGOOD: You're all right, Ernest. You're just not her type.

RIDLEY: Yeh, she says I'm not safe. Too damned right I'm not. If I was safe I wouldn't be in a whore's hotel with somebody's auntie waiting for a meet that smells like a dead cat.

HAPGOOD: Where would you be?

RIDLEY: Anywhere I like, with a solid gold box for a ticket.

HAPGOOD: You can walk away, Ernie, it's only skirt.

RIDLEY: Shut up.

HAPGOOD: (*Cranking up*) You'd better be sure, she plays without a board. You haven't got a prayer.

RIDLEY: *Shut up!*

HAPGOOD: If you think she's lying, walk away. If you think bringing back her son will make you her *type*, walk away. You won't get in the money, women like her don't pay out – take my advice and open the box.

RIDLEY: (*Grabbing her*) Who the hell are you?

HAPGOOD: I'm your dreamgirl, Ernie – Hapgood without the brains or the taste.

(*She is without resistance, and he takes, without the niceties; his kiss looks as if it might draw blood.*)

SCENE 6

The pool. Night. Empty. A towel hangs over the door of Cubicle One (any cubicle).
It is dark. RIDLEY (TWO) *enters from the lobby carrying a large torch. He looks around with the help of the torch. He moves upstage. We see only the torch now. The torch-beam comes back towards us.* RIDLEY (ONE) *walks into the beam. He has come from the showers (depending*

71

on the layout). He carries the sports bag. He approaches the torch. The two men embrace briefly. Our RIDLEY *remains: The one with the torch retires. (The torch, of course, changed hands upstage – here and subsequently we only clearly see, and only hear, the actor who plays* RIDLEY.)

RIDLEY *now opens his holdall, takes out a disc-box and posts it under the door with the towel on it. He removes the towel and enters Cubicle Two. He hangs the towel over that door.*

HAPGOOD *enters from the lobby. She pauses. Timid.*

HAPGOOD: Ernest . . . ?

    (RIDLEY *with the torch, reveals himself.*)

RIDLEY: It's OK. Call the boy.

    (HAPGOOD *hesitates.*)

    Call the boy.

HAPGOOD: Joe . . .

JOE: (*Out of sight*) Mummy . . . ?

    (*He appears from upstage in the cubicle area.* HAPGOOD *moves to where she can see him.*)

HAPGOOD: Hello, darling. It's all right.

RIDLEY: Stay there, Joe.

    (JOE *halts.*)

    Do it.

    (HAPGOOD *opens her bag, takes the disc-box from it, and posts it under the door of Cubicle Two (where the towel hangs). She pulls the towel down and tosses it over the door into the cubicle. She comes back to* JOE *and takes his hand.*)

HAPGOOD: Off we go.

    (HAPGOOD *takes* JOE *out through the lobby doors, followed by* RIDLEY.

    When they have gone RIDLEY (TWO) *comes out of Cubicle Two, holding the towel and the disc which* HAPGOOD *had posted. He takes the towel to Cubicle One, where it had originally hung, and tosses it over the door. The door of the cubicle opens.* WATES *is inside.* WATES *has a gun.*)

WATES: (*Just conversation*) Hey, Ridley. Here's what you do. You walk, you don't talk.

    (WATES *walks* RIDLEY *upstage into the dark cubicle area.*

Pause. BLAIR *comes from upstage and approaches Cubicle One.*
He takes from the cubicle the disc which had been posted there.
BLAIR *moves out towards the lobby but before he gets there*
RIDLEY *comes in.* RIDLEY *is amused.*)

BLAIR: (*Greeting*) Ridley.

(RIDLEY *laughs.*)

RIDLEY: It never smelled Russian, not for a minute. It smelled of
private profit. No wonder the kidnap was so clean. Uncle
Paul. What a breeze.

BLAIR: Except . . . surely . . .

RIDLEY: Except the boy will tell. I'm thinking.

BLAIR: I should.

RIDLEY: There was no kidnap.

BLAIR: Better.

RIDLEY: There was never any kidnap. You and Hapgood.

BLAIR: Much better.

RIDLEY: You and Hapgood. Make it look right, make a mug of
me and the sister, and afterwards both of you back in place
like china dogs on the mantelpiece.

BLAIR: Now you've lost me. Something about a sister.

RIDLEY: The sister is perfect. I know about this. She's here and
she's not here.

BLAIR: I keep thinking you said sister.

(HAPGOOD *has now come in quietly from the lobby.*)

Surely you know Mrs Hapgood?

RIDLEY: I know her sister better.

(*To* HAPGOOD) Don't I?

(*She gives nothing away.*)

Give me a minute, I'm slow.

(*A* RADIO *talks, softly, briefly. It is in* HAPGOOD's *hand. She
raises it to her mouth.*)

HAPGOOD: Mother.

(*The* RADIO *mutters and stops. She puts the radio in her bag.*)

RIDLEY: Listen, be yourself. These people are not for you, in the
end they get it all wrong, the garbage cans are gaping for
them. Him most. He's had enough out of you and you're
getting nothing back, he's dry and you're the juice. We can
walk out of here, Auntie.

73

HAPGOOD: You should have opened the box.

RIDLEY: I could have walked away with it any time and let the boy take his chances. This way you got both, my treat.

HAPGOOD: There was nothing in there except a bleep.

(*Pause.*)

RIDLEY: Well, now I don't know which one you are. One of them fucks and one of them –

HAPGOOD: Don't Ridley –

(RIDLEY *is going to kill her, as promised. Everything goes into slow motion, beginning with and including the sound of* HAPGOOD's *gun, lasting probably five seconds.* RIDLEY *has got as far as taking his gun out when* HAPGOOD *shoots him. Meanwhile,* WATES *is leaning into view, upstage, slightly late, gun in hand. Strobe lighting.*

BLAIR *doesn't move.*

Meanwhile the cubicles are disappearing, and we are to find ourselves outside rather than inside the lobby doors. If the doors themselves remain the sign 'Men' is no longer reversed.

RIDLEY (*i.e. his body*) *is erased along with the cubicles and becomes a body on a stretcher, the face covered by a blanket. The gunshot and the strobe extend through this scene change. At the end of the change we are left with* HAPGOOD, BLAIR *and* WATES, *the stretcher with stretcher bearers, and the* RIDLEY TWIN, *handcuffed, under arrest being led away.* RIDLEY, *passing the stretcher, manages to look at the face under the blanket. He cries out indistinctly and is led away* (*by* MERRYWEATHER).

There is the flashing blue light of an ambulance off-stage. All this happens swiftly, continuously from the gunshot.)

BLAIR: (*To* WATES *angrily*) Where were *you*?

WATES: I was second, he was third.

(*To* HAPGOOD) Oh, you *mother*.

BLAIR: (*To* WATES) I want that ambulance out of here.

WATES: No rush.

HAPGOOD: Ben – ? It was the shoulder.

WATES: No, ma'am.

HAPGOOD: It was the shoulder.

WATES: I'm sorry. It's not like targets.

(*Pause.* HAPGOOD *moves a few paces towards where the stretcher left and then comes back to* WATES.)

HAPGOOD: Ben, thank you for your co-operation.

(*They shake hands.*)

WATES: You bet.

(WATES *leaves.*)

BLAIR: Come on, Elizabeth, Joe's waiting.

HAPGOOD: We said we'd do it without Joe.

BLAIR: It had to look right.

HAPGOOD: You lied to me.

BLAIR: Without the boy it wouldn't have looked right.

HAPGOOD: I was willing to risk it.

BLAIR: I wasn't.

HAPGOOD: I'll never forgive you for that, never ever.

BLAIR: I know that. I knew that.

HAPGOOD: And what am I supposed to tell him?

BLAIR: Tell him it's a secret. Small boys understand that.

HAPGOOD: What do you know about small boys?

BLAIR: Well, I was one.

HAPGOOD: Paul –

BLAIR: No, no, you'll get over it.

HAPGOOD: No.

BLAIR: What about your network?

HAPGOOD: *What network?!* Ridley's blown it inside out! Christ, Paul, I must have been buying nothing but lies and chickenfeed since Joe was in his pram!

BLAIR: One has to pick oneself up and carry on. We can't afford to lose. It's them or us, isn't it?

HAPGOOD: What is? What exactly? The game has moved on. Read the signs. It's over.

BLAIR: Try telling that to the opposition.

HAPGOOD: Oh, the KGB! The opposition! Paul we're just keeping each other in business, we should send each other Christmas cards – oh, f-f-fuck it, Paul!

(*So that's that.*

BLAIR *turns away, hesitates and leaves. The next time* HAPGOOD *moves she is standing by the rugby pitch.*)

HAPGOOD *stands on the touchline. She isn't looking at much.*
KERNER *is standing some way behind her, wearing an overcoat.*
Some rugby sounds.
KERNER *comes down to join her.*
HAPGOOD *sees him.*

HAPGOOD: Joseph . . . You came to say hello?
KERNER: On the contrary.
> (*He looks front, a bit puzzled. Gamely.*)
> Interesting.
HAPGOOD: It hasn't started yet. They're just practising.
KERNER: Oh yes, which one is he?
HAPGOOD: (*Pointing*) New rugby boots. I'm awfully glad to see
> you.
KERNER: (*Spotting him*) Oh, yes.
HAPGOOD: He'll come over when they take their tracksuits off. I
> tried to find you this morning.
KERNER: I was buying my ticket. Also a suitcase.
HAPGOOD: I heard you've been sending your luggage on ahead for
> months. Does Paul know why?
KERNER: (*Shrugs*) Paul thinks I was a triple, but I was definitely
> not, I was past that, quadruple at least, maybe quintuple.
HAPGOOD: They found out about Joe, didn't they? They turned
> you back again. You made up the truth.
KERNER: It is nothing to worry, you know.
HAPGOOD: I'm not worried. I'm out of it now. This is him.
> (JOE *runs in, wearing his tracksuit, which he takes off now. His*
> *rugger kit is clean. The new boots.*)
JOE: Hello, Mum.
HAPGOOD: Good luck, darling. This is Mr Kerner – Joseph.
> Another Joe.
JOE: Hello, sir.
KERNER: Hello. How are you?
JOE: All rights'a, thankyous'a.
> (*To* HAPGOOD) Will you be here after?
HAPGOOD: Yes, see you later.

(She has the tracksuit. Perhaps the top half goes round her neck.
JOE *runs off. Pause.)*

KERNER: Very nice. Very English. *(Pause.)* Of course, he *is* half
English, one forgets that. Well . . . good.

HAPGOOD: Do you want to stay for tea? They lay it on for parents.

KERNER: Better not, I think.

HAPGOOD: Oh, Joe.

(She breaks down. He holds her, awkwardly.)
*Prosty, Josef.**

KERNER: *Da nyet – vyet u menya byl vybar, Lilichka.*

HAPGOOD: *Nyet tagda u tibya nye bylo vybora –*

KERNER: *Da – mu ya pashol . . . ya napishu kagda dayedu . . .*

(KERNER *kisses her and starts to leave.)*

HAPGOOD: How can you go? *How can you?*

(She turns away. The game starts. Referee's whistle, the kick.
After a few moments HAPGOOD *collects herself and takes notice*
of the rugby.
When the game starts KERNER's *interest is snagged. He stops and*
looks at the game.)

Come on St Christopher's – We can win this one! Get those
tackles in!

(She turns round and finds that KERNER *is still there. She turns*
back to the game and comes alive.)

Shove! – heel! – well heeled! – well out! – move it! – *move it,*
Hapgood! – that's good – that's better!

---

*HAPGOOD: I'm sorry, Joseph.
KERNER: No, no. I had a choice too, Lilychka.
HAPGOOD: You had no choice then.
KERNER: Yes, I'd better go. I'll write when I get there.